I0616245

The Great Mass Awakening: Unraveling the Veil of Apathy, Energy Vampires, Empathy, and Ascension

Author: Zoila L.R. Masiak
Published by IAMZROSE LLC

The insights, experiences, and spiritual teachings shared in this book are based on the author's personal journey, divine wisdom, and observations of collective energy. While real-world themes such as apathy, energy vampirism, empathy, and ascension are discussed, this book does not intend to single out or make direct claims about any specific individuals or organizations.

Any references to characters, events, or situations are either drawn from personal experience, spiritual revelation, or general patterns observed in humanity's evolution. Any resemblance to actual persons, living or deceased, is purely coincidental or a reflection of universal truths, rather than a direct portrayal of any one person.

This book is intended for educational and spiritual exploration. The reader is encouraged to reflect, discern, and integrate the material in a way that aligns with their personal truth.

Cover design by: Zoila L.R Masiak

Library of Congress Control Number: 979-8-218-62779-9
Printed in the United States of America

Table of Contents

Preface

The Great Mass Awakening: Unraveling the Veil of Apathy, Energy Vampires, Empathy, and Ascension is a call to action, to deconstruct and a return to empathy. A roadmap for those on their spiritual awakening and a guide to reclaiming your divine connection in a world designed to keep you asleep.

This book is not just a read—it's an activation for your remembrance. It exposes the unseen forces that drains your light— the many masked foe, apathy spirits and energy vampires.

This is especially for the empaths— You've been told your sensitivity is a weakness, but it's your greatest strength. *Empathy is key*— to your gifts, your intuition, your healing, your justice and your liberation.

Zoila, is a true walking miracle. She's been struck by lightning, awakened during surgery, survived open-heart procedures and near-death experiences. She wrote *The Great Mass Awakening* while suffering from a neck injury and the healing journey that took place. She channels Christ Consciousness, her Ancestors, and walks with Spider Woman, Lilith, the Creator, and shares her knowledge of the Great In-Between.

These pages were born from the sacred fire— written with lived truth, and remembrance. There is humor, there is reverence, and there is a fierce devotion to unraveling the veil.

Each chapter carries Zoila's unfiltered voice, sacred insight, and unwavering commitment to awaken the Collective. You'll be challenged to deconstruct, sacrifice apathy and shed societal masks, confront indifferent spirits, and step boldly into your spiritual body and your purpose.

Christ Consciousness is rising and with it, so is the return of *Empathy and the Divine Feminine.* Empathy is not a weakness — it's your greatest gift, compass and keys to bridge the divide.

Dedications

To those who are dedicated to their awakening, and their long journey to self, I apologize in advance. Some of these truths may sting, as the weight of truths can have such an effect. We are indeed living amidst the some of the most interesting times. The Time of *the Seventh Great Mass Extinction* and **The Great Mass Awakening,** a boom of unlimited knowledge, with the capacity to record and observe the horrors in real-time. There is no more critical time than Now. *–Like everything else, a leap of faith is a must...*

May some of these self-imposed, unconventional lessons

and wisdoms be of Service to the Collective and The Great Mass Awakening.

May you call your soul back with every

I Love you!

-All My Love

Zoila

To All I Love

To All I Love,

Thank you to all my Native relations and Elders along the way. So many of you brought remembrance, which I thought was impossible. Thank you for recognizing my need to protect my essence in times of crisis. Thank you for teaching me the importance of Grounding. Thank you for knowing my need and encouraging my return to culture despite the long journey and the continuous efforts to learn and practice. Those few kind words were life changing. Thank you for your advice and truths that pushed me to trust my intuition and visions. Thank you for always being gentle, kind souls who held me up when I didn't even know what to ask. Thank you for seeing me with heart, encouraging me, answering the tough questions, and the much-needed conversations. Thank you for teaching me the importance of Feasting the Spirits and the rigorous need for Spiritual Cleansing. Thank you for holding my hand, though I did not understand the potency of your touch. Thank you to every Native that pulled me to the side, every time we locked eyes; every one of you kept the Spirit of my Ancestors alive within me. Thank you for reminding me to call back my soul. The journey of Remembrance was one I very much needed. May all who know you honor you in all the ways you deserve. May you continue to free others as you have liberated me. May the world forever see you in the light that I see you. May your eyes always dance with joy and strength. May your life and the lives you've touched be filled with abundance, healing, gratitude, and generational wealth that allows for many dreams, blessings, and miracles.

Thank you to all my Ancestors and Elders! May the Veil of Tears and silent cries be heard around the world. May you rest at ease. Your daughters and sons are waking up, dancing, fighting, planting, and uniting once more. May we walk with as much Courage and Resilience as you have blessed us with. Silence no more. We hear you. If you must weep for us, may we make you weep with joy and pride. May peace wash over the masses with the tears that had to rain down your beautiful faces.

Thank you, Mom, and Dad, for ensuring I got as many good, strong, tried, and true lessons as possible. They have been my sword and my shield. Thank you for always holding me to the light with your unconditional love. How much the world needs what you gave so freely. May these lessons touch the masses and help unbind that which torments the souls of babes.

Thank you to my brothers, sisters, and all I call family. The world didn't know what to do with all of us; no way could we be contained under one roof! Thank you for loving me from afar, even though life circumstances took us away from one another. Oh, how my love for all of you gushes and overflows as my heart sings the story of us. May your hearts never be caged, forever soaring as freely as the Eagle.

Thank you to my nieces and nephews. Thank you for looking back and reaching out to me. May you stay as sweet as you are and never let the world change you. May the world rejoice with pride and wonder when they hear your name. May your children be as charming, determined, joyful, talented, and as fabulous as you are.

Thank you to my three sons. Quite literally, my miracles, who kept this miracle from disappearing into the void altogether. If you had not witnessed my life, I might not have believed in my own. Thank you for teaching me so many beautiful and valuable lessons. The love I have for you surpasses all existence of life itself. May your words ring true. May you roar like the ancestors before you. May you blind the world with your light. May the water wash away your fears. May the fires set your heart ablaze, just as you have mine. May the wind breathe new life in the moments you cannot breathe for yourself. May the Mother of us all always welcome you home with full embrace. May the Storms be your greatest teacher and protector, and may you always listen to the Thunder in the distance. May you always know when to duck and cover and when to push through. May the Sun forever shine in your favor. May your lives be filled with abundance, joy, glory, and grace. May your journey North be smooth sailing. May you take as many as possible, and do not fret with whom you cannot.

We all have choices. We all have lessons. It won't be easy but fearlessly remember who you are and who you are not, and it will make for less chaos.

I love you to the end of the Universe and Back. The three of you have been my breath and the very reason is I continue to breathe. -All My Love, Mom!

About the Author

Zoila is an Author, Artist, Mother, and Shamanic Practitioner in Southwest Va, she is a Natural Healer guided by her Yaqui and Jewish Ancestors. A child born with her heart wide open, raised by Kings, Queens, Clowns, and touched by lightning. Baptized and initiated by Death's unfortunate lessons and equally graced with Life's miracles. Surviving many battles, defeats, self-imprisonments, and having experienced a variety of great divides. A warrior of another kind, surviving open heart surgery, 10 pacemakers, numerous TIAs (transient ischemic attacks), PEs (pulmonary embolisms), multiple congenital diseases, countless NDEs (near-death experiences), and more. Many of her spiritual abilities and gifts were developed through the most extreme situations. The separation of the soul from the body has been some of the most isolating and equally the most blissful and freeing experiences of her life.

Her father, a worldly and profound thinker, born in 1931, was a 101st Green Beret Airborne Veteran, who served in the Korean War, the Japanese Occupation, and two tours in Vietnam. He was an engineer, medic, pilot, photographer, an engineer for Jacque Cousteau, an avid chess player, a jazz lover and a philosopher of his own making. He was called "Sarge" by everyone who knew him. Her mother, born in 1943, is known for her beauty, creative talents, grace, joyous nature, and generosity. To many, she was a second mother. There was never a stranger; instead, others were met with acceptance and unconditional love.

Zoila spent her first five years primarily in the hospitals, with surgeries and a medically induced coma. Though she experienced extreme confinement and a sterile environment, she was lucky enough to be born to parents who embraced and encouraged her sovereignty. Zoila is the youngest of eight. Her early years were spent playing and roaming freely along the marshes of Guinea. A small town in Gloucester, VA., known for the hardworking watermen and for their old-world attitudes and dialect. In the 70's and 80's, the community was less diverse, and outsiders were often viewed poorly by the locals. However, they embraced the Masiak family. The elders of the fishing community taught her family how to make crab pots, and gill nets and to work the waters. Today, her siblings own and operate crabbing businesses serving the Richmond and Tidewater Region of Virginia. Her family is known for their charming, gregarious, and hardworking nature.

As a young girl, tragedy struck her family once again with the sudden death of her brother, Peter. A drowning took his life as he tried to save another. Peter was loved and known for his charismatic, joyful, and fearless nature. His death undoubtedly shaped the lives of all who knew him, as he was a hero to many.

Named after her mother's before her, Zoila Luz Rosario Masiak is a name not frequently heard. Her name is as peculiar as her lived experiences. One does not often think about the uniqueness of a name; however, the name "Zoila" has always made others question her ethnicity, identity, and citizenship. Many times, out of curiosity, other times because of fear. The struggle of growing up in the South with such a name has been a genuine cause for problems, as otherisms' afflicted many of her interactions.

Her name has always played a significant role in her life. The reason for such uniqueness comes from the fact that both sides of her family were victims of forced assimilation, holocaust, and genocide. By the 1900s, there were less than 5,000 Masiaks worldwide and less than 5000 Yaquis of Turtle Island. Numbers that would reflect extinction.

Both sides of her family were part of the European expansion. Her European roots can be traced to the first settlers in the Americas. On her mother's side, her grandfather's family was the first and second wave of Spaniards who colonized Mexico and the southern hemisphere. On her father's side, her grandmother's family can trace their roots to the first protestant settlers. While different parts of the hemisphere, both sets of grandparents were disinherited for marrying those of ethnic and Indigenous backgrounds. Consequently, both sets of parents were not raised with their extended family, and both sides left their home area to protect their children from the slights of being considered interracial marriages at the turn of the century.

Her first name comes from her Great Grandmother who was of Spanish descent. Zoila (pronounced like Soy-La) means full of Life or Of Life, or IAM The. Her middle name, Luz Rosario, belonged to her Tia and Great Grandmother of Yaqui descent. Masiak is from the Polish-Jewish side. While there is so little history of her last name, the pronouncing of her last name is close to, Mashiach, the Hebrew word for "Messiah". Her name loosely translates to I AM The Rose Colored Light Messiah or Life of The Rose Light Messiah. Her name could not be more fitting, as it is every bit of her nature and, she is, indeed, the definition of a walking miracle.

Chapter 1: Personal Truths

"Open Heart Warrior" ©*Zoila Luz Rosario Masiak 2017*

Throughout my life, my multi-dimensional and multi-talented aspects are often confused by most. It has left me isolated like the bubble girl with a curious back story. My *be-ing* frequently does not reflect my untold battles, as my joyous and kind nature tends to precede me. Often making others believe, I know not of any suffering.

I was not born with the privilege of knowing "good" health; as I was born with four holes in my heart, seizures and surgeries were frequent as a child. The memories of anesthesia wearing off and waking up during surgeries, being resuscitated, or being an experiment are beyond imaginable, even for me. I was a very traumatized little girl who experienced horrors no child should go through, and I struggled with selective mutism. As the body, mind, and spirit can only handle so much stress before it detaches itself.

I remember as a child, holding Christ Conscious memories and being very spiritually gifted and prophetic. In fact, I couldn't set foot into a church without being filled with overwhelming grief and rage. The nightmares of seeing Christ on a cross, were much like my own, though it was scapples and not thorns. I saw him as being perpetually humiliated, not letting him down from his suffering. Punished for his empathy and gifts and for flipping tables to those who chose to oppress. I could never grasp the cruelty. Praying for empathy from others around me and wisdom so that people could hear me, my silent cries, to see me, to know that they were causing me pain. How could they not know? This was at the core of my rage. I assumed everyone knew empathy as I did, and I didn't understand that they were not self-aware or fully conscious.

In my teens, I stopped dreaming. What dreams I did have, they were sporadic. These were very dark times for me. I was constantly in trouble in school, bullying, fights, drinking, I had lost my brother, grandmother, and grandfather, and in my mid-20's, I lost my father. My attempts to end my life failed me, and in truth it made me feel like a failure as well. The birth of my children, while challenging, saved me from me. Rather than obsessing over the ways I suffered, I was determined to raise them with as much empathy as I could muster and no masks. I never wanted them to feel the confinement of masking and shielding their light, as I had.

From the time I was 18 years old to 35 years old, I struggled with DVTs, pulmonary embolisms, and mini strokes, as I went undiagnosed with a genetic clotting disorder, EDS (Ehlers Danlos syndrome) and the fourth hole was never mended.

I struggled with my weight for the first half of my adult years, and every time I had a clot, I would develop CHF complications. I was stuck in a negative feedback loop. The PEs would have me sick for 5 to 6 months out of the year, and I would gain roughly 40lbs in the winter, losing 20lbs through spring and summer. In my 30's, my weight peaked at 370 lbs.

Auto-immune complications, fibromyalgia, CSF leaks and complex migraines were my regular for over 20 years. Dysautonomia had me to the point where I could not walk very far, and I needed a wheelchair to be in public. The most humiliating thing for me was when I could not bathe myself or even shampoo my hair. I had dreads for 7 years to maintain my independence and dignity. I was faced with the reality that I simply may not be around for my boys, and I had to heal up. My healing journey started with tackling my food and alcohol addictions, then my personal relationships and the relationship I had with myself.

The night I left my ex-husband, my dreams started flooding back. I had spent months with reoccurring dreams, and I became committed to my healing and to following my visions. Even if that meant leaving everything and everyone I knew. In the past ten years I've lost 200lbs; though it has been the spontaneous healing that confirms my knowing and it was the second lightning strike that quite literally lit a fire under me. I knew I had to straighten up and fly right, that some of my truths would inspire empathy in the hearts and minds of those willing to sit and listen. Oftentimes our experiences and truths are not humble. They are hard and heavy realities. Though harsh, this is where we alchemize and turn lessons into wisdom. – *Water into Wine.*

Pain in the neck

When I embarked on my journey to heal up, I never thought about writing my knowledge down. I have always lived outside of the societal norms. I spent more time in the marshes and with the wild things than I did with my own peers. Domestication has never been my best subject. My parents and family failed miserably at it. Perhaps it was because I am the youngest of 8 or, because of my heart condition or because I was encouraged to do my own thing. While I can do a great many things, I have always been outside looking in. I often joke that I don't know time, *only divine timing.* Living in flow with my creations and the rhythm of the seasons. The idea of "time" has always been vague and illusive to me. Far easier is it to be in communion with the plants and animals or to raise children than it is to really understand the concept of "time." As you can imagine, my way of *be-ing* goes directly against much of societal teachings, making me unnaturally sweet and an unintentional thorn to some.

The spring of 2023, I had finally returned home after years of being a way. I attended a wedding believing, the outside would be safe. I have several food allergies that cause me to have anaphylaxis. Between my own healing and the years of COVID, I really missed my family. I had brought nuts to get by, because there were no accommodations regarding foods that I could eat. I was horribly wrong. I was not prepared for contact anaphylaxis.

The day after the wedding I was in full body hives. They were everywhere, my abdomen, the palms of my hands, my eyelids, even the bottom of my feet. I had kept myself safe by staying away, but I was not prepared for the hugs and kisses to cause so much damage. I spent a little over a month in that state with gastric distress. I lost close to 40lbs in a very short period. I was about a month into my hives when it hit me, just how much rage I had been feeling. I turned to my ancestors and started intentionally turning down the heat within my mind. I realized that while the hives were not great, I had made my suffering longer than needed, simply by returning to that state of rage that I thought I so diligently removed and gotten control of. The hives cleared up within a few days once I realized I had to cool down.

The rapid loss of weight coupled with EDS, made my port sink into my heart. It felt like having a toothpick poke the inside of my heart and I couldn't breathe deep, nor could I talk too much without experiencing extreme pain. It took me a few visits before the doctors agreed to take it out. When they did, I told them my history of EDS and that I have a history of waking up during surgeries. Well, guess what happened? I woke up during my port surgery. Amale surgery technician got scared and he placed his hands on my head, leaned a lot harder than he needed to and told me not to move. After surgery I was sore but ok-ish. However, I think I was just excited that it was over. Adrenaline does that. Like having a car accident, you do not realize the damage until a few days later. The day after surgery, I was outside enjoying the fresh air, and it felt like I had another TIA coupled with chest pain and a feeling like my head snapped off my neck, it felt like I had to hold my head in place. Obviously the worse came to mind, but I knew I had to stay calm to the best of my abilities. It was very treacherous times for me, as I was continuously being mishandled. One Hospital accused me of being an undocumented immigrant seeking pain medications, another hospital berated me for not walking or eating. It was a very devastating time for my children, as the fear of losing their mother loomed. I was fumbled and mistreated by many that I encountered. Long story short, I survived despite the poor care that I received during that time.

I started writing because of this devastating neck injury that left me incapacitated for nearly three months. I could not talk without extreme pain, nor could I bathe myself, walk or eat. While I had known pain, this was the first time I had experienced so much pain that it felt like it would never end. It was in that time of experiencing a great divide that I turned to my light and ancestors to heal myself. I honestly believed I would not make it, and I wanted to share my knowledge with my children and the collective, because I know my truths would inspire others to return to self. As you can imagine, it is astonishing to not only survived but to walk away with a book in hand and wisdoms to share. Indeed, it is a blessing to be here; to share some of my story and wisdoms I've learned along the way.

Truths are not humble

Walking with my dad was like walking beside a king. Everywhere we went, people parted ways for him, and everyone was eager to speak to my dad. He was one of those brilliant men who believed everything could be self-taught and he had a photographic memory. When people would ask, "How's it goin,' Sarge?" He always had a grin and would respond, *"It's your world. I'm just passing through."* It was he who taught me that our minds are infinitely vast, and that no one had authority over my *be-ing.*

He would often say, *"I fought wars for you darling, so you wouldn't have to."* Though as a kid, I thought he meant literal wars. In my own healing, I realized just how much Dad taught me so that I could be as free as a bluejay, unbothered by others' opinions or projections. Someone else's opinion of me wasn't my right to know, for that would be invading their world. If it were important enough, they would speak up. Dad made the detachment an art form. However, it was my mother, who was art in motion.

One of the more brutal truths my dad, Sarge, would say was, *"50% of the world will hate your ass, and the other 50% won't give a damn. You'll be lucky if you meet one person who accepts you."* While it was painful to hear as a teen, it prepared me for the world of apathy, which I would most certainly have to endure. How people treat you when you are at your lowest, shows you exactly how they feel about you. Simultaneously, those who were with you at your lowest aren't always there when you start to elevate, and sometimes their silence is violence.

Bottom line. Don't take it personally. People can only perceive you at the depths they perceive themselves. Do not believe their lies. This is how you break your own heart, by accepting others' truths as your own. By rejecting the projections of another, it will reduce a lot of your internal stresses and pains.

Most of the time, adverse reactions has everything to do with their internal world and dialogue. Those who pass their judgment out are just that, "passing gas," but from their mouths. You just happened to be the person they let their slight but deadly fumes of apathy escape to, *"Like an old fart, you wave it away"*- Nana, Alejandrina Encinas Dominguez.

Actions speak louder than words. Choose those who reciprocate the efforts you put forth. Those who support and uplift, especially when times are hard. These individuals will be your closest allies. Accepting the hard truth and *"As-Is"* of any moment makes it easier to discern where you should be and how to move through with grace.

Learn to dance with negative energies when people show you their apathy. Side-step and keep moving forward. Much of our domestication keeps us in a place because we fear being rude, lacking manners, or being seen as bad. Equally, if they show a truth that hurts, then that is your trigger point that you must deconstruct, come to know, understand, purge and release. The sooner you can identify your triggers; the sooner you can differentiate your energies from others.

"There are two types of people. Those who talk about people and those who talk about ideas. In this home, we are idea people." -Sgt. John Albert Masiak. Those only consumed by the lives of others offer minimal solutions. They create and participate in more nightmares than sweet dreams.

Keep yourself grounded and do your best to avoid unnecessary drama. *"Believe nothing you hear and only half of what you see."* - Nana, Alejandrina Encinas Dominguez. You are not required to listen to anything that does not move your Spirit. Use your discernment and *Free Will* wisely. If you stay observant, you can avoid most of it, simply by not going along or agreeing with another's choices or perceptions.

As my grandfather would say, *"I heard you the worst time"* -Tata, Federico Gastelum Dominguez. Avoid entertaining such foolery if someone shows you their apathy and untruth that hurts your Spirit. Believe them the *"worst time."* Obviously, you can only sometimes choose to walk out the door. However, when you have a door to exit stage left from, use it liberally.

Respect space. Respecting the space and the sovereignty of another is bare minimum. By respecting the space of another, you are also respecting the space for yourself. Like driving in traffic, it gives everyone room to make mistakes. This allows you to avoid an accident, slow down, brake if you must, or take another route. It is okay if your path does not stay on the same path as someone else. Both are invaluable. The moments in each other's lives often come into being because there are lessons to be learned and a need for grace. Lessons are to teach you to react quicker, become more robust, and to share your knowledge so it is easier for the next.

"Perception. Perception. Perception. It is always perceptions." - My mother, Zoila Blanca Masiak. You cannot control others' thoughts or actions. Let go and just let it be. Letting go of something you cannot control allows for growth and will enable you to create space for those who care for you deeply and authentically. Simultaneously, you cannot let the process of letting go and the practice of detachment drive you to apathy. Detaching from your expectations allows you to accept someone as they are. You free yourself and you free them. There is a balance you must walk. Empathy allows grace to move through you, so you may be the embodiment of grace and miracles.

"Stay as sweet as you are, don't ever let the world change you," was my mother's mantra. Without a doubt, I did exactly that even if it was out of spite at times. As a child my mom and I would walk to the neighboring creek, picking wildflowers, herbs, and blackberries. My mom would

often remind me of how loved I was. For my parents undoubtedly loved each other, and so did their parents. I was made up of nothing but love. I was precious and truly a walking miracle.

She also would share with me how all land was sacred and hallowed, for there was not one inch of soil that had not seen bloodshed. In that way, I was constantly being watched over and cared for. It always encouraged me to walk gently, treating each step as if it was sacred. – *This is what it means to Walk in Ceremony*

When you think about it, the odds of being born human are astonishingly rare — so rare that it's almost unfathomable. The combined probability of everything leading to your existence is estimated at 1 in $10^{2,685,000}$. When you think about the absolutely perfect conditions for you to evolve and survive, and the amount of ancestors, it took for you to experience life, in this lifetime. – *That is the miracle.*

Lessons from Death

Death has been by far the greatest of my teachers. We are not taught how to die, and in that we are not taught how to live fully alive with all our senses, holistically and with empathy. We do not celebrate and give gratitude as we should. We create mourning simply by not celebrating. Even death should be celebrated and rejoiced. Sure, loss is hard; but when we celebrate their lives, we celebrate our own lives as well. – *The Light at Birth, is the same as the Light at Death.*

In short, we must also learn to live and die with dignity and grace. When faced with those last seconds, they feel like an eternity. You must keep calm, have courage, and focus on all the joys and every bit of the bliss and breathe in the light. If you are full of fear and anger, those will be your last moments. Eternity of sweet dreams or an eternity of nightmares. Here is where I felt I had a choice to return. So long as I have a choice, I choose to be here. Though I cannot deny, the Light of Source is as equally blissful as it is isolating. To be alive, in union with my vessel and my spirit, has got to be the greatest of *all* adventures.

In those moments I have found that this world and the gift of Life is the vacation from eternity and having gratitude for the beautiful chaos that birthed such life. It makes being alive just that more glorious and sensual. You only have one vessel, and you are only alive in the *Eternal Now.*

Cherish it. Don't wait until your last breath to have wished you had fully lived...

Deconstruction

Throughout my life, I would spend a lot of time deconstructing words and their ideas. Doing this, I realized that in my own deconstruction, this is how we break spells. One word in particular that has always held me captive, and ironically it has also set me free. The word, *disease.* A term I had heard from everybody around me, and it was how I described myself. A constant state of disease and suffering.

Let's deconstruct, *to be Diseased.* (dis) -to be without, (ease) - to be comfortable. To be *dis-eased* means to be without ease. Well, surely, I know what it was like to be uncomfortable, and I know those horrible moments do not last. I have come to know that being without ease is temporary. Everything is. Any given moment passes as quickly as it comes in. Learning to breathe and taking care of your spirit during the tender moments is vital. – *This too, shall pass; though it may pass like a kidney stone, it will pass.*

The day that this came into my mind's eye was the day that my fibromyalgia started to decrease. Rather than focusing on all my pain, I focused on all that I enjoyed and appreciated. What I could do versus all that I could not. I discovered that I was quite capable of healing myself. I leaned into my spirituality and my gifts; I started experiencing spontaneous healing.

My complex migraines are no longer daily events, fibromyalgia disappeared, dysautonomia flares have all but ceased, the hump in my neck vanished and a fist size mass of scar tissue from the pacemakers in my youth, in my abdomen shrunk to the size of a quarter. I am not limited to wheelchairs or days on end in bed from the crippling pain or fainting spells. I must admit, I found it quite humorous that much of the pain that I was experiencing most of my life was simply because I was not listening in and actively ignoring my gifts. Surely, there was nothing funny about it in those years of pain, though today, I find divine comedy in it all.

Healing is not linear, and most certainly not singular. Try not to bite off more than you can chew. Give yourself adequate time to deconstruct, digest, process and integrate.

Chapter 2: The Evils of Apathy

" Evils of Apathy "©Zoila Luz Rosario Masiak 2021

"*The Evils of Apathy,*" a vision I had in 2014 and painted in 2021. In this period of significant personal turbulence, I had gone nearly 10 years without painting, and my creations ceased abruptly. I had made a monumental agreement with myself that I would return to the land and paint once I felt I could breathe, and my spirit could thrive once more.

A lifetime of tower moments and winds being continuously knocked out of my sails, figuratively and literally, had me nearly crippled. As one cascade of unfortunate events happened to be my normal. I've always made a note to listen to the visions that invoke so much rawness — the ones where I am as lucid as I am while I sit here with my cup of coffee in hand. These moments are the ones that drive my leap of faith. My visions pushed me to move my family and myself to the Appalachia's before the pandemic hit — A region that continues to teach to those who are willing to listen. –*And listen, we must.*

Through the Eyes of Spider Woman

In the vision I found myself at the feet of the Original Woman, the Original Dreamer of Dreams, Spider Woman; the healer and the dreamer of the hearts of humanity, the one who speaks with the Mother and the one who speaks to her children. She was the first to observe and heal herself of broken bones and diseases. The girl-child left behind because blindness had made her an extra mouth to feed.

Her cries were those of a veil of a thousand tears. Her wail was more powerful than the harsh gale winds of the winter northeastern storms. Her heartbeat was louder than any beating drum. Her eyes were white and cloudy with blindness and old age. Her hair was matted but somewhat organized with bones and shells. Her hands, while strong, were gnarled with time. Her skin was copper brown, like the muddy clay she remembered as a child. Her old tough skin, speckled in scars and tattoos, told tales of her unnaturally long life.

I looked at her and she gifted me the ability to look through her eyes. She shared with me the first time she saw her hands; muddied by the wet clay of her heavenly infancy and shared the best years of her life, the mud pie making years. She shared the Light of the Creator that brought her down from the Stars, *and the Light of Birth was the same as the Light at Death*. Most importantly, she shared her reflection in the water. Water often reveals self-awareness and consciousness, to those brave enough to look and to those who can survive its depths. It was undeniable. Her consciousness was confirmed.

I did not know her name then, but I knew her rage and sorrow, the wail only a heartbroken mother makes at the loss of her child. Though these tears of hers were for all the world's children, her grief was like no other. Standing in a cave before Spider Woman, I fell to my knees by the weight of her pain. In her sorrow, she shared a glimpse of the past, her nature, and her unending grief.

She shared the future of extremes: earthquakes splitting continents, ecological collapse, economic collapse, extreme droughts, famine, deep freeze, untamable fires, lightning raining down with a vengeance, pandemics, raging storms, tidal waves, wars, melted ice, a collapse of the polar ice caps, the stagnation of waters, mass migration of all beings, widespread disease, and unfathomable death. Lightning sparked horrendous fires, melting cities to the ground. The fires were unmatched since the heartbeat of the sea didn't pulse with its once harmonious rhythm. Like any other diseased body, our Earth Mother was inflamed.

41

Spider Woman showed me the loss of beaches and marshes that would decimate the coastal regions. Cities would wash away. Working against the sands of time, the powers that be, believed they had more power than She, Our Earth Mother. Rather than moving the people out of danger, many without sight could not tell they were being led to their extinction. The suffering was unimaginable.

She told me that we had to migrate just like our ancestors did, with the lessons of survival passed down through the ages. We had to leave, as we would not survive an economic collapse, pandemics, storms, and erosion.

She shared with me the Veil with its infinite masks, *The Evils of Apathy*, which tortured the children and devoured the essence — everything from children to grass to celestial bodies. *The Evils of Apathy* oozed of nothingness, black and gray sludge with an insatiable appetite that could never be satisfied, dripping with the unforgettable stench of burning and rotting corpses. With each mask leaching onto everything and everyone; like a parasite, it takes hold of minds, worming its way slowly, hardening the arteries and the heart. It finds its way into every corner, crevice, and body that invites it in. Purging Apathy out of every corner of your vessel is paramount to life itself. Revolution will be inevitable as we cannot survive Our Mother's death.

A period of renaissance will be born, bringing in a bio-technological boom with regenerative systems based on an egalitarian, moneyless society, with a return to the land and food foresting. A return to honoring the water and the way of the Mother. — *True Matriarchy*.

The First to Awaken

The Great Mass Awakening will be a mass collective consciousness, with millions of communities strong, placed in a grid linked in the most extraordinary ways. Magical reverence and the supernatural returned with the ability to commune with all *be-ings*. Some call themselves angels, children of the sun, chosen ones, diamonds, dragons, empaths, rainbow children, star seeds, two-spirited, or werewolves. No matter the name they call themselves, these beings are multi-faceted, full of Light and overflowing with empathy.

They are composed of artists, architects, creators, healers, survivors, and warriors of all kinds. They bridged the divide between the worlds, creating a network of resources, food forests, medicines, safety, and shelter. Their Light broke the spells that chained the masses, dispersing the illusions of the Veil, and were the keepers of the *Dream of Dreams*. Many prophecies are coming to pass. – *The Time is Now*.

These Light beings chose to hold their innocence and sweetness close to their hearts. They are the first to return to empathy, return to innocence and return to the way of the Mother. They are the lighthouses for the storms created by the nightmares. The nightmares chose Service to Self only.

The first wave were the anchors, architects, and key holders of *The Great Mass Awakening*. They had to wake up from their nightmares and begin to clear the fog and smoke between the mirrors. They had to be everything apathy was not. They had to denounce all the entities that made their souls and bodies scream. For what makes them cry, scream and quake is the same for our Earth Mother.

They must spread as many seeds as possible, even if only one takes fruit. Learn to commune, conserve water, grow indoors, herbalism, healing, and remember a time when we lived with the Spirit of Our Mother. If we wish to return to the land, Apathy cannot take our bodies, hearts, minds, and souls.

They had to decolonize their minds to the point that it drove them to meaningful action — the actions that course corrected the misdeeds of the past. Acts filled with unconditional love and empathy connect them to each other and all the *be-ings* in this world. They must be the embodiment of empathy, grace, and Service to Others. Service to Others means for us to be the caretakers to one another, the Earth Mother, and the Miracle of Life.

Service to Others was not meant to enslave children into generations of unending Apathy. Our Mother was not to be pillaged, as if it did not take billions of years to create the most perfect and precious conditions for life itself.

The Long Road to Remembrance

"I AM The Anthesis to Apathy: The Journey Home" © *Zoila Luz Rosario Masiak 2023*

The dreamers who dreamt the Dreams of Dreams their entire lives or for a very good portion of it felt a great loneliness, though they often shared a single heartbeat. Many who have an abundance of Light in their bodies have had some of the longest and hardest paths full of significant obstacles, suffering and oppositions; alone and with a heavy cross to bear. Their bodies and hearts were bruised and burnt by unfathomable betrayal and grief.

These beings will have many positions, and many will have more than one mission. Composed of architects, artists, builders, dreamers, healers, some tend to the land, music makers, shields, and warriors; all are Creators. Unfortunately, they initially could not know each other, as the entire world needed them at the same time. They had to create a net that could handle the weight of the world.

Indeed, the task would break the backs of those not strong enough. Their Will Power had to be Supernatural. Their Light felt galaxies away as the Children of the Sun woke up and danced once more, calling forth the ancestors to step into their vessels. These Children of the Sun in serving justice starved the many masked foes; the *Evils of Apathy,* giving way to seeds of new life to sprout.

They would know one another in due time. Much work had to be done alone in the dark, as there was no other way to know the enemy. They had to first wake up, heal up, heal the generational trauma that binds them, and remember Remembrance. They had to tackle the nightmares to lead others through the fog. In their healing they would awaken those around them. Like a tidal wave, there is always turbulence, undertowing and washing away of the sands of time before the shores are calm enough to build again.

They had to deconstruct all illusions and the structures that upheld the nightmares within themselves and the external world. They must turn their backs on the nightmares, no longer having the luxury of playing with their past tormentors. They had to wake up and dream once more. Ultimately, the greatest of all tasks was to decolonize, ridding themselves of Apathy, colonization, and indifferent spirits. These Light Beings would eventually show up, suit up, soldier up and take on the undaunting task of Remembrance and a return to the Earth Ways. — *A Return to Innocence*

Eventually, conscious communities would emerge; full of creators, dreaming and creating solutions. While Our Earth Mother purges and the powers that be who are filled with apathy go to war, these light beings must avoid panic and head North. They had to stay safe and do their best not to accept the nightmares. - *The solutions are in the Sweet Dreams…*

Dual Paths: Liberation and Remembrance

A return to the land means a return to Indigenous knowledge. We must honor and respect the sovereignty of all Native peoples of the world. Native people have been and still are the fiercest defenders and protectors of Our Mother. They hold the longest living Remembrance. The Elders, women, and children are by far the most precious. Their existence has been chained by unfathomable cruelty, brought on by forced assimilation, colonization, and continued genocidal practices; from the very structures that passed off their bloodthirsty death cult as; glorious, virtuous, civilized, moral abiding dogma.

The task will not be easy. There are so few native people today, making up less than 6% of the world's population. The needs are enormous: forced assimilation, boarding schools, broken treaties, colonization, forced detribalization, forced sterilization, ongoing genocide, human trafficking, and war on their lands and waters. Their very existence hangs on by a thread. They are indeed the endangered ones. They are the elders, messengers, and teachers still with us today. The dehumanization of Native peoples worldwide directly reflects the actual sickness that plagues Our Mother. They should be allowed to exist without fear of genocide, eugenics, or inhumane treatment.

The task of returning to the land could not be done without the courage, leadership, stewardship, truth, resilience, and wisdom of Native Peoples worldwide. Raising the voices of Native peoples is paramount, as their leadership is key to our survival. Native peoples must be at the forefront and have authority over every decision regarding animal rights, human rights, land, mineral, water, and resource acquisitions. Everyone must take a pause and listen to their cries.

May their cries make us so uncomfortable that our stomach turns, letting bile hang in the back of the throats, unable to avoid until it drives meaningful actions toward liberation, redistributions, reparations, sovereignty for all Natives, the survivors of boarding schools, and their descendants. — *None of us are Free unless we are ALL Free!*

The Placenta. The Womb. The Shield.

Courage, resilience, and resistance are not generational curses passed down by our ancestors; they are the greatest gifts our ancestors bestowed onto us. They are the requirements for an unbreakable

Willpower. One must push through, just like our ancestors. The sins of our fathers have pained us far too long. No more can we let their "logic" lead us, as it has led us far away from our children, hearts, and land. Their egos, logic, and need for control have borne a world oozing and *dis-eased* by apathy. Our vessels were never meant to be confined to concrete, genocide, and war.

Now is the time for mothers to rise to the undaunting task. Mothers must stand up to Apathy. Mothers must rock the boat. Mothers cannot be the ones to torment their children; otherwise, too many will perish from the weight of Apathy. Mothers must respect the autonomy and sovereignty of a child's vessel. Mothers must not be the ones who steal the breath away from their children or teach them how to be violent to other *be-ings*. Mothers must teach the gentle embrace of all the senses.

Mothers are sacred vessels that create angels from their blood, bones, sweat, and tears. Mothers teach their babies boundaries and safety. Mothers teach the babies acceptance, harmony, and unconditional love. Mothers teach creation, dance, laughter, play, and the ability to transmute difficulties. Mothers teach their children how to heal themselves and those in need. Mothers are the ones that build community and make it a home. Mothers remind us to be good brothers and sisters to one another and to be good children to our ancestors and elders. Mothers must also be good sisters to one another. This is what it is to be a Mother – *The Placenta. The Womb. The Shield.*

Chapter 3: State of Be-ing

"Rocky" ©*Zoila Luz Rosario Masiak 2023*

It's funny how simple observations of life tend to hold so many wisdoms. I came to understand the concept of being a *"Be-ing,"* by sitting in silence with nature, specifically with the chickens that share the land with us.

Though they have an established coop that they return to every night, they roam freely. As I watched Rocky, one of our roosters, a beautiful and regal Dominique, his black and white iridescent feather sparkling with hues of blues, greens, and purples, radiating his magnific- ent strength, as he proudly stood guard; there he was, not a care in the world. Just standing there, being a chicken, sovereign and mighty. How simple and sweet his short life was. No debts, dogma, townships, or obligations were other than to be a chicken. I sat there, coffee in hand, observing him scratching the ground. There he was, glorious, strong, and proud — *his nature, his instinct, his Spirit.*

Just like Rocky, we are all *be-ings* experiencing the same ground, sun, wind, and water. To be a human, means we are *hue-man*, a *be-ing* made of light and matter. Our light is vast and infinitely expansive. As *hue- mans*, we are aware of our consciousness, with the ability to observe the consciousness of others and the ability to create stories and manifest with intention, which makes us different. The greatest fallacy in our *hue-man- ness* is our incredible ability to reason. The capacity to reason gives us the ability to justify the most inhumane acts, and the other side of that is the absolute surrender to unconditional love.

The same ingenious electrical spark that beats our hearts and allows blood to course through our bodies is the same one that brings forth the mind's electrical impulses into action. That spark is our consciousness, making divinity known. That spark is what sets our souls ablaze. That spark allows us to dream and bring forth from our minds to create with our hands and to share our stories. That's the magic of the *hue-man be-ing*, a *be-ing* made of light and matter, with the ability to consciously create. Making us both the threat and the solution.

Nature, by far, is the greatest of all teachers in that anything and everything has a state of *be-ing*. When you spend time in silence and with those other *be-ings*, you come to know their instinct, their nature, thus knowing their Spirit. In this way, our world is a massive library of simple truths.

One of the simple truths passed down to me through my Nana, Alejandrina Encinas Dominguez, *"There are only ever two lessons you learn from those around you. You either learn how to be or you learn how not to be."* It is effortless to learn all the ways of how *not* to be, and many will gladly show you a world of despair, hopelessness, nightmares, and pain, disconnecting you and leading you away from your path and purpose.

When something upsets your internal compass and directly opposes your Spirit, it will be felt throughout your entire vessel. This is the key to tuning in. Observing what negatively affects your body teaches you empathy, how to identify and recognize needs versus wants, what to avoid, what to do if presented with similar situations, and how to help those in need when able. Asking your higher self, is this your truth or not? If it is not your own, you can sidestep and move forward. Sticking around for others and situations that go against your essence will burden your body, heart, mind, and soul. You are not required to walk the same hell as others to learn the lessons. — *This is precisely why Empathy is Key!*

The Mind is Its Own World

"La Luz Rosario" ©*Zoila Luz Rosario Masiak 2023*

One cannot presume to know anothers' way of *be-ing*, as we are not experiencing the same realities. We are merely just passing through, learning lessons from one another. When there is acceptance of the fate of flying by another but not holding tight to the energies in your body, the accepting and casting of projections are significantly reduced. Giving a sense of freedom to another, as they are not bound by spells and the projection of your mind.

You may be on the same path with another for a while, and your paths may diverge. Accepting the divides is part of the resilience to keep moving forward, as we all must walk the long journey to Self and Remembrance alone. Empathy is key to the bridge between all the realms and all the worlds.

We, indeed, are a world of our own. Our minds are vast in experiences and expressions, giving way to lessons, knowledge, and wisdom. We all have the ability to entertain and observe much information, with the capacity to enter different states of emotions and consciousness and we can do so intentionally. Therefore, you must realize you are never the center of anyone's world. The center of anyone's internal world is their own *be-ing*.

Knowing you are of this nature; you can begin to see the importance of choice. The power of choice is your indistinguishable Willpower. *Free Will is the Muscle of Choice*, that creates, guards, and protects. With intent, the potency of your actions and words magnifies.

Everyone has a vast internal world and experiences that are unique to us. You are your own world; you are not privy to another's thoughts or feelings. Even if another shares and you can feel them, we are still our own world and the main characters in that world. As you can only truly ever know yourself. So, if you must be stuck with yourself, you might as well treat yourself with the same admiration, grace, and love as you would for a child and be your own best friend.

Anytime you try to read another's energy without them giving express verbal permission or an invitation, you are impeding on the sovereignty of another. You have no right to wonder what anyone thinks of you, nor do you have any space to presume. If they want you to know, they will tell you. If they do not share, that is okay too. It is an invasion of their world to presume to know what anyone feels or thinks because, in those moments, you start to project your Will onto another. By not taking part in the projections of another, it frees both parties of any unnecessary energetic chains that bind.

Your mind can only live in one world at a time. You cannot sit in the once-was, could'ves, should'ves, or would'ves at any given time, nor can you stay in that space with others and the same goes for living too far in the future while also maintaining focus on what you are doing. These brief moments of distractions are where trickster spirits and parasites seep in. These are the moments of potential soul loss and accidents, knocking you off track.

Free Will gives you the strength to push through as well as bliss and creation. Free Will allows you to choose authenticity. No masks required. — *Free Will is the Muscle of Choice, one that must be exercised liberally.*

The Powers of Attention, Creation and Focus

"Lupita" ©*Zoila Luz Rosario Masiak 2022*

Where you place your focus is the world your conscious mind resides in. In this way, you can move through time, space, and worlds if you hold focus. Giving others your time, focus, and intent allows for the most impactful experiences for another to receive. Staying in the now keeps you safe from accidents, natural disasters, parasites and predators alike. It also aids in the ability to dream the solutions and quicken the time needed for healing.

Your mind can create heaven, or it can create hell; simply by creating distractions and nightmares or creating sweet dreams and solutions. Choose the solutions, as they often serve more than your needs alone. This is the divine magic of your *hue-man-ness*. Creating with your hands from which your mind imagines. In this way, you embody what it means to be a Creator. — *You Co-Create with the Creator.*

Co-Creator

The *Great In-between* is where the Creator speaks to you. The in-between is the state of surrender, the neutral bliss that I have come to know; we are all Creators, and we Co-Create with every breath we take. We are made of light and matter, sparked by lightning; the flames project and reflect and like water our consciousness flows through us and outside of us. Creation is our natural, ingenious gift to the world.

The Creator can only create. To a Creator, everything it creates is sacred. Authenticity, unconditional love, synchronicities, and vibrations is how the Creator speaks to all its creations. The Creator can be heard, through the multitude of synchronicities and vibrations. Giving freely and aiding those who are willing to listen.

Synchronicities are deeply personal observations and interpretations. Everyone experiences this differently. An example would be praying for a miracle, seeing angel numbers and shortly afterward, your prayers were answered.

Another example: for myself has come by way of memories of my ancestors. In my home, the Fall is synonymous with "tamale time". This is the time when the days become shorter and we spend our cold nights indoors, deep in thought and in remembrance. I usually make molé outside over an open fire to prepare for the tamale making. In my return to the land and with efforts made, so has much of the life. The birds of prey have been the most spectacular, confirmation of what I know to be true.

The past few years, when I've made molé over an open fire, the Eagles would fly and dance so high in the sky that I could barely see them with my naked eyes. In my experience, as a Child of the Sun, in these moments, the Ancestors and Creator are very close by. Downloads, personal epiphanies, and remembrance tend to follow suit.

Chapter 4: Mirrors

"Hue-Man Mirrors" ©*Zoila Luz Rosario Masiak 2023*

As a child, I was obsessed with my observations; that a leaf was the same pattern as branches, the branches were like that of a tree. I saw this in all things and believed that this was of all Life. My father installed a screen saver that had endless fractals. I was mesmerized more by the infinite loops than the games. Granted, the old IBMs we had in our home didn't have too many games at the time. And before there was the world wide web, our school had installed a "new" computer lab, and the computers had been networked together, but certainly not like they are today. The moment I realized this inter connection, I saw the inter connections of all of us, all that is, and thought our neurons must be the same. And if that were so, then surely our universe would have infinitely branched out and infinitely branched inward, like the fractal on that black and green screen of our old IBM floppy drive computer. I believed then, as I do now, that our empathy is one of our most valuable gifts. Empathy allows us to truly experience, *feel* the world around us and the ability to commune with all *be-ings* and there would be a day when the world would know each other in such a way.

All life expresses itself in such a manner. Like crystals and trees, they are mirrored reflections of larger bodies. Though, there is no perfection in replication, only in that replication is perfection. You see, we are all mirrored facets of Source. You are the observer, observing what it means *to be* alive. You are of the Creator and our Earth Mother alike, both Light and Matter. You are Divinity making *itself known.* For even the Light is blinded by its own light and requires clear mirrors to fully observe itself and its depths.

You are your own world, with your own experiences and expressions; thus, you can never truly know another person's world. However, if you know empathy, you can feel another. With empathy, you can understand the needs, and you can be the one who moves forward and offers Grace. It calls in more than just your thoughts and words. Your intentional actions become very potent. In this way, you embody what it means to be a Miracle.

The Birth of Mirrors

In your first months, your survival is solely contingent on the Acts of Service provided by your caretakers. Mirroring is the natural course of learning and observing, as it is for any being. "Research has shown that our brain has a specialized group of cells called mirror neurons, which is responsible for empathy and compassion." (Orloff)

A newborn can only see about nine inches away from themselves. That is roughly the distance from your eyes to theirs, while breastfeeding. As newborns grow, so does their scope of vision and the ability to observe. In those first few weeks, through these windows of the soul, placing our attention and focusing on their innocence and needs; we share our light confirming their existence and beginning the first steps of self-awareness, the transfer of consciousness, and programming.

As a mother, I have come to know that the art of painting the world with my eyes for my children. The ability to transmit such a world and has allowed the gifts of empathy, telepathy, transmutation, and the ability to unmask with ease as there is less requirement to mask.

Masking Mirrors

Masking is the unfortunate side effect of being forced to hold back your inner light, and the inability to move energies out of your body; forced *"to be seen and not heard."* The more you are forced to mask, the more pain will be stored in the body, shortening, and stripping away your life force, *your essence*. Your authentic self is the *one* who wears no *masks*. Your Light is undeniable. It has the ability to shift energy in spaces before you even enter a room.

It is an unfortunate side effect of modern circumstances that many do not mirror the same light back to their children; that children come into this world possessing. This ability to reflect a child's light back to them is the most valuable skill in developing and strengthening empathy. Instead, they imprint their perceptions, binding them from the beginning. This is quite painful to a tender infant who is new to being a *hue-man be-ing*. As they know not of any judgments or pains of this world.

How you care for, nourish, protect, speak, tone, and pitch all matter, as your voice becomes the infant's first internal dialogue. You also share your essence through the breath, and your eyes paint the tapestry of consciousness and focus. You teach them about the external world by how you respond to their needs. The sounds of the larger world can be very alarming to a being coming into their own existence.

As caretakers, you must care for babies in a holistic manner, teaching them not only to be aware of their physical bodies, but the senses, their consciousness, their energies, their spirit, and that of the external world. Giving them Grace and room for their autonomy and sovereignty.

To be in Hell, is to be out of the sight of God. What are the consequences of not sharing your Light? What type of hell are you enforcing on your children? What happens if you do not honor their autonomy, and sovereignty or mirror the light back?

They know not what they are. These are the first layers of the veil. This is the Hell, the internal battle of one's own existence, for you have been blinded, and cannot fathom that you are burning and burning all that you touch.

Smoke Between the Mirrors

Without proper mirrors, you only look down at your body, seeing your feet, hands, and legs; even the tip of your nose is vague. You cannot fully grasp how the outer world sees you or perceives you and you certainly cannot see the entirety of your physical form without clear mirrors. The same applies to your spirit, self-awareness, and consciousness. So often, what is being projected back to us is another's internal hell and not the light.

If you agree with others' perceptions, you unwittingly take on the "perceived" version that is not your own. Believing these false truths about yourself can manifest into your internal dialogue, inherently stripping you of choice and *Free Will*, forcing the body to disconnect, mask and shut down.

Free Will is the Muscle of Choice. One that must be honored and nurtured. Like any muscle, it must be exercised often and vigorously. It is a daily exercise of *Free Will* that shows up as choices, lessons, and tests. Remember, *there are only ever two lessons, how to be or how not to be.* You will be presented with similar lessons, until you learn discernment.

Agreeing to perceptions that are not your own will create energetic chains that bind, and smoke will cloud the sight. Accepting false perceptions will force you to turn against yourself, betraying your own heart. This pain can be the deepest wound to heal. As they are inflicted in the most unassuming ways. Having a healthy doubt of what the world tells you is not a bad thing.

Words can mask intentions; however, empathy moves thoughts and words into action. When the actions and words match and are reciprocated, it improves communication, discernment and has the potential to uplift. Just like animals, if you know anothers' instinct, you will know its nature, needs, and you will come to know its Spirit.

Shielding Mirrors from Smoke

Infants and children are full of light, producing more light than they drain. However, their needs are the greatest, consuming more energy, and they must be met with Grace and tenderness. Like all animals, you learn through the eyes of your mirrors. From the eyes of an infant, they look up to their Creators.

Denying children, the light from your eyes, and sharing cold and indifference instead, you begin to teach them the meaning of Hell. It is through your eyes that you observe the world. Where you focus, your light follows. Children are both the absolute best and the absolute worst of us, reflecting our truths onto the world.

Children naturally move energies through their bodies, but over time, they lose the ability when society demands them to be seen and not heard. Social niceties will always demand you to override your own bodily autonomy. When children are not encouraged to move their energies through their bodies, it interrupts their ability to recognize their own spirit, and if they cannot recognize their own energies; it makes it harder to recognize that of the other *be-ings*.

Children are the future of us; modern society must shift its consciousness and begin to consider the ramifications of denying children their autonomy and their sacredness. Teaching the practicality of deep self-awareness, emotional intelligence and introspection allows you to lead with empathy. These lessons of empathy teach you that all Life is as valuable as your own and just as conscious as you are. Knowing your energies, you come to feel, know, see, hear, smell, taste, perceive and sense the energies of the world around you.

The world is loud and abrupt compared to the womb. The Mother's state of being during this time is as vital as the infants. Those first seven years are best filled with nurturing, gentle touch, baths, and soft tones. All eight of the senses: sight (visual), taste (gustatory), touch (tactile), hearing (auditory), smell (olfactory), vestibular (balance), proprioceptive (movement), and interoceptive (internal), must be engaged with heart and intention.

By doing so, it teaches them to know their four bodies: emotional, mental, physical, and spiritual and how to engage in the world in a gentle and respectful way. As well as to respect their own boundaries and a clear difference between what is of themselves and others — creating the understanding of empathy without learning it through force or trauma. In these gentle in-betweens, you will come to know empathy as one of your most precious and valuable gifts. Those gifts grow throughout your lifetime.

With enough time, spiritual gifts develop and can be applied to everyday life. A way to expand experiences and self-expression. Tools to sit in your sovereignty, free from emotional, spiritual, and mental intrusions of others' illusions, and it allows for direct communication with your higher self, and all that surrounds you and Source.

This ability allows for healing, insight, knowing, purpose, wisdom, and directions to the evolution of self and the realm in which your vessel dwells. These abilities allow you to develop relationships with any *be-ing* in a more connected way. You develop the capacity for clear intuitions, creations, and solutions when you operate from this state. — *The shared state of mind, is communion.*

Consequences of Media's Mirrors

Mirroring is how all beings come to learn how to be. All parts of the world can be received and mirrored back to the masses. Media is the most apparent form of mass energy exchange and control. Unfortunately, our society has become numb to a certain level of trauma and toxicity. Thus, we cannot see the damage to our children in the long run.

In today's world of extremes: extreme individualism, sexual gratification, and extreme violence are accessible and instantaneous. At the same time, the rate of human suffering and human trafficking on a global level is at an all-time high, as well as the destruction and suffocation of our home world. — *The Mother of Us All.*

Energy Vampires have always used media of all kinds for broadcasting and programming. Those who are in the entertainment business understand how important it is to gain and retain the audience's attention. The industry is ruthless. Few make it, without being consumed and left with but of a husk of who they used to be. Just look at any child who has entered the entertainment business. It is no coincidence that many experience extreme horrors and lose themselves in the process. — *All that glitters, is not gold.*

Those who create and influence mass media have always told us: who and what they are; and what they do to children, the minority, and the vulnerable. Look no further than the 1915's film "Birth of a Nation," the 1938's radio broadcast, "War of the Worlds," or the 1940's film "Pinocchio." In "Birth of a Nation," you will find the glorification of the ideals of a white knight, saving the damsel in distress from the blackfaced man, wearing their white hoods and burning crosses. In Pinocchio, there is a scene of whispers where they speak of "pleasure island." They take all the "bad children" and lure them in with the ability to "do whatever they please," hinting at human trafficking while they slide a bag of coins to one another. The loss of life caused by mass suicide in the 1938 radio broadcast, "War of the Worlds" is confirmation of the power of mass programming and mass "psyops".

Mass media has always been a tool that drives rapid consumption, consumerism, fear, individualism, and grand escapism from the chaos and nightmares they created. Before radio broadcasting and films, it was the Churches that wielded the power of "knowledge" and drove people to madness and nations to war.

Media sold to the people the glorious, sexual prowess and the powerful life of vampires, as if it were something to aspire to. Before the sex appeal of modern films and novels, they were the definition of evil. Feeding off the children and women with ease. Those who are the very lifeblood and the heartbeat of humanity. It is no coincidence that men like Ebstein and more have been accused of some of the most heinous acts against humanity. They are the "entertainment" business after all.

When society no longer looks to the windows of the soul as mirrors, and mirroring screens instead. That is all the proof you need that humanity is indeed suffering from being disconnected.

However, modern social media, like TikTok, has allowed many to observe themselves in a more honest light, the ability to mirror one another, connect and share their consciousness in a more authentic manner; driving information away from mass media shareholders. The realities of this world can no longer be distorted or swept under the rug. We are witnessing the effects of rampant energy vampirism in real-time on a global scale, something we've never experienced and hold no human memory of.

Fractured Mirrors

"Soul Loss" ©*Zoila Luz Rosario Masiak 2025*

When you experience trauma or any exaggerated outburst of energy, you experience brief moments of *soul loss.* Not all soul loss is traumatic, such as fits of laughter or orgasms, as the French would call it, "le petite mort," little death. Your breath is how your spirit travels. It is the loss of breath; brief moments of loss of consciousness and disconnection that cause soul loss, which leaves your vessel open for potential trickster spirits or parasitic attack. Everyday activities like laughter do not require too much work. You just ground yourself and remember where your vessel resides.

Depending on the nature of the event will depend on the severity   soul loss. NDEs (Near Death Experiences) are more apparent reasons for soul loss. However, accidents, anesthesia, alcohol or substance abuse, illness and starvation and products of extreme violence such as abuse and war, can cause soul loss as well. Sexual abuse and physical abuse are more common experiences. Emotional and mental abuse will also lead to soul loss, especially if it is unrelenting and there is little time for rest and recovery.

Soul loss happens when you experience points of fracture of your spiritual body. In these moments, part of your soul removes itself to protect you from the pain of what is happening in your physical reality. Soul loss is not the loss of your soul completely, but fragments of your soul that are no longer in your vessel. Like a rubber band, it can becomes stretched too far, to the point of snapping. All manners of *dis-eases* and shadows make themselves known when your light is not fully present.

Imagine that you are holding a glass of water, the glass breaks and water spills in every direction. The glass represents your spiritual body. The water represents your essence, emotions, consciousness, and memory. Most of the pieces of glass are close by for you to pick up; but inevitably one or two little pieces of glass go flying far away from its container, your vessel. So yes, you are there, but there are also some vacancies.

Your body may age, but the trauma will settle into your fascia, muscles and joints at the age the trauma occurred, making you rigid. Trauma can be direct or indirect and become fixed into your emotional, mental, physical, and spiritual bodies. Many times, the emotional and mental bodies will get stuck at the age of when the trauma occurred, making it exceedingly difficult to heal and move forward. This is where the soul loss can be very damaging and soul retrieval will aid in your healing.

When there is soul loss, you may feel a sense of dissociation, loss of time, feeling stuck in autopilot, functional freeze, imposter syndrome, numbness, and more. These are the points of access for *dis-ease* to set in and over time, will manifest into physical illness. While you cannot control outside forces, it is vital that you do not let these energies settle into your bones.

Just like there is a *Spectrum of Light*, there is also a *Spectrum of Grays*. When the Spirit leaves the body, it gives room for the parasites to worm their way in. From the point of sight, from which you view the world, it becomes clouded with fog and smoke. Another layer of the veil that will require you to deconstruct, cleanse, purge, transmute, and heal. So that you are not unintentionally burning those outside of you.

When you are not entirely in your body and your consciousness is not in the *Eternal Now*, this is when Trickster Spirits play. Simple accidents like spilling coffee, tripping over your feet, walking into a branch, etc. These moments are the signs that you are not paying attention to your vessel and all its surroundings. It is imperative that you keep focus on one world at a time.

When your focus is *not* on your vessel or its surroundings, this will lead to parasitic entities, like anxiety, fear, or rage. These are the moments where you are spooked easily or lash out. You can even experience a full walk in. Where you are not yourself, and sometimes you can be consciously aware that you are not yourself. Your behavior can be very extreme. It can be quite confusing during these moments, which perpetuates a negative feedback loop. It could be either your ego, your shadows, your ancestors, or even energies that you are not familiar with.

When you are in this fog, your body will develop all manner of *dis-eases*. As the body becomes stressed and unrested, your immune system becomes depleted, and your hormonal system will also be affected. All four bodies need proper rest, nutrition, oxygen, movement, and hydration.

As you work through your healing journey, it is also very crucial to work through your ego, shadows, personal demons, ancestral and generational trauma. You will discover that the ego isn't the worst. It is your fiercest protector. As it is the masks that guard the inner child and innocence. However, it is when the ego is the front seat driver and self-awareness, and consciousness are not driving your vessel; that your ego will run amuck. As you work through your shadows, you slowly clear the vessel of any fog and smoke, making way for the light, for your spirit to return home, and to remember who you are. — *Not the trauma. Not the pain. Not the programming. Not the projections.*

Your spirit is quite sweet and does not like to hurt. It is your spirit's way of protecting you from additional pain and from spiritual pain as well.

72

Remembrance and the Return to Self, is the Self Actualization and Ascension, Rebirth and Resurrection of your *be-ing*. The innocent self, the sweet self. That is your Light. You came into this world knowing the Light. The Ascension process is the return of your essence and operating from a higher state of awareness, magnification of your Light and the driver of your vessel. This state allows you to be the walking embodiment of unconditional love, empathy, grace, and miracles.

Chapter 5: Empathy is Key

"Empathy is Key" ©*Zoila Luz Rosario Masiak 2025*

Empathy vs. Sympathy

Repeatedly, these two get crossed. Many believe empathy is the same as sympathy. They are quite different, and here is why. "Empathy is the ability to recognize, understand, and share the thoughts and feelings of another person, animal, or fictional character. Developing Empathy is crucial for establishing relationships and behaving compassionately. It involves experiencing another person's point of view, rather than just one's own, and enables prosocial or helping behaviors that come from within, rather than being forced." (Alexander, Jean.)

"The difference between Empathy and sympathy is found in how we relate to the other person. Empathy is shown in how much compassion and understanding we can give to one another. Sympathy is more of a feeling of pity for another. Empathy is our ability to understand how someone feels while sympathy is our relief in not having the same problems. " (Psychiatric Medical Care Communications Team)

There are times when sympathy is an appropriate emotion for a problematic situation. However, sympathy can create distance from the person struggling. Sympathy is the greatest of apathy's deceptions. The empty, forced, and habitual use of *"I'm sorry"* and *"with sympathy,"* marked on everything from cards to T-shirts, bringing in a plethora of untold amounts of money to companies. These are prime examples of how sympathy can be bought for less than a dollar.

As widespread as sympathy is, it does not allow for meaningful action. It offers no solutions, nor does it allow others to hold space or safety for those who need support. It often diminishes your ability to feel supported enough to ask for help. For some, guilt, fear, judgment, shame, or being pitied becomes more significant than recognizing the need to seek help. Sympathy does not allow you to be the embodiment of Grace but instead the embodiment of a hands-off approach — *apathy*.

Empathy takes it a step further. It puts thoughts and prayers into action while honoring an individual's sovereignty, creating a space for unconditional love that allows individuals to be the walking embodiment of Grace. Empathy gifts us the ability to recognize the needs of others. When you act on such needs, you create opportunities for miracles to manifest every time you pursue actions of Grace versus actions of indifference.

Compass

Empathy is key to your all-knowing, intuition and your antenna to Source. It is your multi-functional antenna and compass that allows you to know: all four bodies, how to detect diseases and to heal yourself, how to commune with other *be-ings*, to know the natural world, the ability to know all four directions, which way the sun rises and sets, the moon placement and the seasons, the approach of a storm and how to stay safe, where to find food, shelter and water, how to find and produce medicine, the ability to receive and interpret your dreams, synchronicities, and more.

Empathy allows you to truly feel what others are feeling. It is an inherent skill that must be fostered. The feelings of others can be emotionally confusing and physically painful, especially for children. It is the ability to sense others' pain, so you do not have to experience the same lesson twice.

Just as *Free Will is the Muscle of Choice* and authenticity is your Light at birth; empathy is a gift from Our Creator, as well. Gifts so you may recognize, move forward or side-step situations that may be harmful as well as to aid and uplift the world outside of you. It is the internal knowing that you do not want others to suffer as you did. It is a trait that keeps you safe and allows you to look for and tend to the needs of yourself and outside of yourself. More than pain and suffering, it is the key to your emotional intelligence, compass, connection to Source and all your spiritual gifts.

Dreaming

Empathy allows you to *inner-stand*, and it acts as a guide while you dream and meditate. When you fall asleep, your body is left unattended. It is quite a vulnerable state if you think about it. In your waking hours you have a lot of control over your vessel, but not while you are asleep. Your body is just there. Your consciousness and your spirit never really rest. They go to Dream World, the astral realm. Here, you can traverse a wide variety of extraordinary realities.

When you are a child, dreaming is usually full of hope and play. As you grow into your vessel and strengthen your consciousness and spiritual awareness, you can learn to control your dreams. The ability to be aware of your dreams allows you to manifest your dreams into reality, to find solutions, visit your ancestors, and spirit team. You can even visit those you love, and others can visit you, too.

The Dream World is quite infinite, and it is key to your infinite potential. As you learn to navigate through Dream World, you will find that it gives you information about the present, past, and future, as well as how to prepare. Learning to control your dreams is a skill that will keep you safe.

The inability to hold focus can cause you to get stuck in nightmares, and experience spiritual attacks or sleep paralysis. While nightmares are quite scary, they cannot fully hurt you unless you allow it. Learning to control your consciousness even while you dream will enable you to swiftly move through the planes. If you experience too many nightmares, they will keep you from being fully rested, and you will start to manifest nightmares in your mundane reality. You cannot entertain nightmares and sweet dreams at the same time. Sweet dreams are where you find solutions; nightmares, on the other hand, will take you far away from your path and purpose.

Higher Vibrations

In my mind's eye, empathy is even a higher vibration than authenticity and unconditional love. Unconditional love is easy. It is accepting people as they are and not who you wish them to be. Holding space for their existence and the sovereignty for all that is them. Knowing, they too, are made up of the same Light, and bleed red just as you do. We have far more in common than our differences. — *The Oneness of Us All.*

Authenticity is your sovereign state of *be-ing*, your birthright and Light. However, it is Empathy that is an even higher state of operation. *Empathy is the key,* your compass, justice, intuitions, and spiritual gifts, and drives you to meaningful action. – *To be fully alive is an action.*

Authenticity is often viewed as a higher vibration because the closer you are to your authentic self, the closer you are to your inner child, the easier it is to remember the Light, as that is what you come into the world knowing.

However, a person can be authentically awful, cold, cruel, and apathetic and claim they are being their authentic self. Likely they are being the version of themselves best suited for their preferences. Empathy is an even higher vibration than authenticity because it drives your vessel to intentional actions. Actions that have the potential to uplift yourself and all those around you.

This is what Christ was trying to teach. The ability to heal and ascend go hand in hand with empathy. The return of Empathy is a Return of Christ Consciousness. Everyone has the ability, though you must choose and maintain the Light. The choice to be sovereign or to be sleep-walking, is your choice and your choice alone. This is the double edge sword, of Free Will, because to be fully awakened while others sleep can be painful and lonely. As those with empathy are often not heard by those who are burning and projecting apathy into the world. The Creator can only give you choice, it cannot dictate it, for dictating you would strip you of your inherent *Free Will*. The Creator can only create and observe, our vessels are the tools to which we manifest and our consciousness is the bridge.

Genuine empathy is more than the ability to feel your fellow *hue-man*. It is also your compass that keeps you healthy and safe, the ability to commune with all the *be-ings*, elements, dream realms, spirit realms, ancestors, and connection to your Higher Self, Source, and the everlasting Heaven within. Empathy allows Grace to move through you, aiding in the ability to be the walking Embodiment of Miracles.

Too often, empathy is viewed as your greatest weakness, when in reality, it is the heaviest and sharpest of all your tools aside from *Free Will*.

Justice

Children's innocence isn't just filled with bliss, imagination and wonder; it is filled with a keen sense of justice. Children cannot fathom the wrongs of this world, as they cannot observe the broader scope. Because of this, justice is quite simple. Children inherently grasp when something feels wrong. Through examples of empathy, you teach them whether their plights will be ignored. Giving birth to what they acknowledge and observe, gifting them their first set of keys.

As babies, when you see or feel injustice or when in need, your internal alarms scream and screech. They call alertness to the larger world above, that they are in need. The alerting of infants calls their caretakers and elders to act gently and swiftly. Without words, their cries are heard and their needs are met. Their creators come in tenderly, with kisses from the sky. In that moment, all becomes peaceful once more. From an infant's point of view, their caretakes are larger than life and move from a place of being above their small bodies. As we grow, so does the scope of our observations and the nature of calling in our Creator and ancestors. We move from reaction state to intentional invitation.

When you have gentle mirrors, you can connect to the world in a more authentic, dynamic, and energetic way. It is the neutral state of mutual exchange. Understanding even the basics, you will be able to discover the Spirit and needs of other *be-ings*, from infants to insects and everything in between.

Nature's Library

In my mind's eye, humans have always held many states of consciousness and the ability to slip in and out, depending on what you are focusing on or not. Knowing the actions, habits and instincts allows you to understand the alert state, the bliss state, the caged state, the fawn state, the fright state, the flight state, the hunger state, the shared state, the need state, the neutral state, and the emotional body, mental body, physical body, and spiritual body, as well as the sovereign consciousness of any *be-ing*.

Empathy aids in your discernment abilities, and over time, you gain practical knowledge in knowing the energies that drive the *be-ings*. With enough observations, our natural world becomes an unending encyclopedia of simple truths, allowing for practical movement with periods of precognition enabling you to avoid unfortunate circumstances and natural disasters.

Key to Spiritual Gifts

Empathy is key to all intuitions, all the claires, and psychic abilities. Empathy is the key to creation, discernment, observation, innovation, *inner-standing* and it allows for the exchange of energies. These are not gifts for self alone. Empathy is the antenna, compass, your multi-functional GPS, and intuitions; gifts from the Creator so that you may tend to your vessel, one another and the world around you.

These gifts allow you to sense your vessel's needs, the needs of others, a sense of justice, and a guide for intentional action. The potential is limitless. These gifts enable us to connect to one another, the ancestors, the elements, and all the *be-ings* of this world. It allows you to create with your hands from what your mind imagines. Before there is any physical manifestation, it begins with the electrical impulses of the mind. This is the magic of our *hue-man-ness*. Divinity making itself known. Every time you create, you become a Co-creator with the Creator.

Empathy is key to your intuition and all spiritual gifts. Everyone has spiritual gifts. We are all students, teachers, and masters of our own internal worlds with the ability to self-actualize and be of service to those in need. The purpose of these gifts is to tend to one another and the needs of our Earth Mother.

The Ojibwe people of the Great Lakes have such teachings and knowledge. "After the Clan System was given to the people, the Seven Grandfathers sent seven spiritual beings to Earth to clarify who the Clan System was to be used and to amplify the meanings of many gifts often taken for granted in life. The beings came to the people out of the water. They brought many teachings meant to sharpen the senses of the people. It is said that the first five beings brought messages pertaining to the five senses of man: touch, smell, taste, hearing, and sight. The six being brought teachings about ah-mun'-ni-soo-win (intuition) — a special sense that goes beyond the ordinary senses. It was the special sense that goes beyond the ordinary senses. It was a special sense that few people recognized in their lives." *(Benton-Banai.* The Mishomis Book: The Voice of the Ojibway. *pg.78)*

Spiritual gifts have practical uses as well. Take, for instance, Astral projection, which can give you the ability to handle extreme stress or pain by flight from your body when the pain is beyond bearable for your mind to handle while also staying observant. Precogniessence will aid in quick decision-making requirements, such as to prevent an accident or to dodge a disaster. Grounding will keep you in your body and make it hard for those around you to knock you off your feet. All these gifts give you the ability to move you to action and to keep you safe.

The 9 Spiritual Gifts of Clarity

Your spirit requires a vessel and is dependent on the sense to be fully engaged to traverse this physical plain safely. Every part of your body receives information from the outside world. When an empath is tapped into their intuitions, they will have the ability to read both their internal and external world with increased clarity. There are a variety of spiritual gifts, such as charm, discernment, and magnetism. However, these gifts are of the senses. Empaths are naturally gifted in one or several of these abilities. Though, everyone has the potential to learn and strengthen their skills.

Clairalience

Clairalience is an ability to perceive *scents or odors* that are not physically present — such as smelling the scent of a loved one who has crossed over and is no longer with us in the physical world. As well as the ability to smell diseases, illness, or malintent. Those with clairalience are extremely sensitive to perfumes and heavy odors.

Clairaudience

Clairaudience is the ability to perceive *sounds*, voices, or messages not audible to the ordinary human ear. Those with a clairaudience can hear guidance from the physical realm and the spiritual realm. High pitch ringing in the ears can indicate that your higher self or your guides have a message for you. Those with clairaudience may suffer from complex migraines as frequent noises, electrical sounds, radio, traffic, and wi-fi can disrupt their connections.

Claircognizance

Claircognizance or *"clear knowing"* involves the intuitive or instantaneous understanding of information, facts, or insights without the need for logical reasoning or external evidence. They are guided by a strong gut feeling or a deep sense of knowing that doesn't come from logical reasoning or prior information. Those with claircognizance may suffer from anxieties, imposter syndrome, feelings of paranoia as they are sensing incoming energy but no verifiable information, as they are "knowing" and yet not fully informed at the same time. It is paramount that these individuals learn to know their own energies and not to invade into anothers' world too much. Respecting space will deter a lot of unwanted negative energies.

Clairempathy

Clairempathy is the ability to sense the *emotions* of others without being told how they feel or use of apparent signs. Those with clairempathy have a heightened emotional sensitivity to others. They can notice emotional nuances, even when people are not openly expressing their feelings. While clairempathy can be a valuable gift, it can also be challenging, as it may lead to emotional overwhelm or difficulty distinguishing your emotions from those around you. Learning to set healthy emotional boundaries is vital for those with this ability.

Clairgustance

Clairgustance is the ability to receive messages, and insights, by way of *taste*. They can taste the malice or indifference of food that is served to them. Those with clairgustance may struggle with food sensitivities. Eating and preparing food intentionally is especially important to these individuals.

Clairsentience

Clairsentience is the ability to experience *clear feeling,* and sense energy, emotions, and information from the spiritual realm. Clairsentients are attuned to subtle vibrations and emotional shifts, often serving as mediums who channel messages from spirits, guides, and higher realms through physical sensations or intuitive knowing. Those with clairsentience may experience sensory overload frequently, a feeling of being drained when their senses are being bombarded, and frequent headaches.

Clairproprioception

Clairproprioception is the ability to receive information and insights through tactile touch, as well as through the hair. Individuals with this ability can pick up on subtle impressions and energetic shifts by physically feeling them through their bodies or when they come in contact. Those with clairproprioception may experience discomfort or unease in heavily industrialized or energetically dense environments, as these areas can overwhelm their heightened sensitivity to vibrations and subtle energies.

Clairprecognition

Clairprecognition is the ability to perceive or gain knowledge about *future events* before they occur. This can be through dreams, downloads, meditations, or visions. Those with clairprecognition may struggle with anxiety and speaking their truths as what they are perceiving has yet to happen. These individuals may struggle with anxiety or a fearful state of mind or an overwhelming sense of dread. It is especially important that they learn to ground, as future events are always a potential, not yet a certainty. It is a slippery slope to traverse if you are too far ahead, your vessels can be prone to accidents when you are not fully present in your vessel.

Clairvoyance

Clairvoyance, or *clear seeing,* is the ability to perceive information, objects, events, or images beyond ordinary human senses. Oracles, seers, and psychics have this ability. Those with clairvoyance may struggle with frequent distractions, grounding and being fully present.

Chapter 6: Empaths

"Awakened Empath" ©*Zoila Luz Rosario Masiak 2025*

Empaths generally have a higher-than-average emotional intelligence. They struggle with their surroundings, as most energies are not their own. It can be confusing and painful. In part, because society tells empaths to ignore their body and their intuitions. It is quite easy for empaths to feel taxed from the outside world, as they are feeling and observing more than the average person.

Many times, Empaths need clarification with the sensory input that occurs. This is due to the disempowerment, devaluing and ignoring the feeling of the internalized alarms and triggers of their vessel. It causes unnecessary *dis-ease,* distraction, distress, and pain. While tricky to navigate, empathic abilities allow for spiritual gifts and talents. Learning to hold healthy boundaries is quite challenging when you are taught to ignore all your internal alarms. However, once you are aware, it becomes easier to hold and maintain healthy boundaries. You also must hold yourself accountable and be a healthy advocate for yourself.

Empaths often have a keen sense of justice and feel compelled to step in and help. This is because Empaths have some awareness of their sixth sense. Usually, they cannot physically stomach the suffering of others. Establishing discernment and firm boundaries is paramount to protect empaths from being drained. Empaths and children are the preferred prey of energy vampires. Healthy boundaries are vital for anyone; however, an empath must take extra care.

Empaths have the innate quality to make others feel at ease. Their light is undeniable; animals, children, plants, and those needing to be heard, tend to find their way to empaths. Very often, the light they emit is precisely the healing that is needed and is exactly what irritates the parasites in others. Like moths to a flame. It can be quite intense if you are unaware of your abilities as well as the inability to discern and hold your energetic boundaries.

Empathic Burnout

Empath burnout occurs when an empath becomes emotionally, mentally, and physically overwhelmed by the intense energies they absorb from others. Because we are natural mirrors, empaths are susceptible to the emotions, thoughts, and environments around them, they can quickly become drained when they fail to effectively manage or shield themselves. This exhaustion may manifest as emotional overload, physical fatigue, illness, inflammation, irritability, and a sense of detachment from oneself.

While empathy offers profound insights, it also brings heightened sensitivity. Many experience sensory overload and energetic bombardment, particularly in environments dense with unbalanced or apathetic energies. Those not attuned to their own vibrations can unknowingly act as energetic vampires, drawing off the empath's energy.

Empathic burnout is a very real dilemma and cause for many *dis-eases* in a world that teaches you to ignore your body and its plights. As we are not taught to know empathy and all the requirements to tend to our spiritual bodies.

Empaths often struggle with setting healthy boundaries, which leads to constantly absorbing the energy of others, further depleting your reserves. While empathy is important, it becomes unhealthy to have empathy with no boundaries. You will suffer greatly if you constantly over give.

Unconditional love does not mean unconditional boundaries. If anything, you teach yourself to ignore the all of you, and you teach others to ignore your plights as well. How you show up for yourself is how you teach others to treat you. This is why they say, "the road to hell is paved with good intentions." You are not meant to burn indefinitely for another. By overextending beyond your limits, capacity and inability to maintain, you also strip the other person from learning valuable lessons.

Empaths tend to be givers, and even givers have their limits. You cannot maintain anothers vessel and spirit for them, you can only inspire. There is a balance you must foster for yourself and those around you. It is especially important that you learn to know what is of you and not of you. Set firm boundaries for yourself and for others. You must honor , maintain and respect your vessel and its needs. By doing so, you also respect anothers needs as well.

There are many distractions for an empath. As an empath you must know thyself and learn to distinguish what is yours and what is not yours. The unseen world and the extra ordinary experience while full of wonder and adventures, it can also be draining to hold focus on too many worlds at once. Empaths must learn to ground fully, purge, transmute and develop good spiritual hygiene practices. It will help you maintain your energy when faced with energies that attempt to drain you. In fact, I would say they will help you more than anything else.

23 Types of Empaths

Empaths are diverse, each carrying a unique connection to the world around them, yet they are similar in their profound ability to feel and absorb the energies of others. The 23 types of empaths I have observed so far, is intended to serve as a blueprint for understanding the multifaceted nature of empaths.

Animal / Fauna

Animal/ Fauna Empaths understand the needs and wants of animals. They can communicate telepathically with animals, by receiving downloads and epiphanies, the ability to heal and enchant animals. Some may even experience the same pain in their bodies when they see an animal hurt. Animals tend to flock in their direction, as the magnetism pulls and relaxes the animals into a neutral and shared state, rather than a reactive and fearful state.

Claircognizant / Intuitive Empath

Claircognizant / Intuitive Empaths have powerful intuition. Intuitive empaths can enter a room for the first time and immediately sense the underlying vibration of the people and the present situation. They tend to have knowledge that surpasses their education and firsthand experiences. Intuitive empaths have the keen ability to aid in the healing and safety of those around them. Some may struggle with gastric sensitivities, as intuition is often felt in the gut.

Cognitive Empath

Cognitive Empaths possess an extraordinary ability to understand the thoughts and mental processes of others. Unlike emotional empaths who feel the emotions of others; cognitive empaths can recognize and interpret the thoughts, beliefs, and mental states that influence behavior. This type of empath is highly perceptive and can pick up on the motivations and intentions of those around them.

Collective Empath

Collective Empath are deeply attuned to the collective consciousness of humanity or a specific group. They are extremely sensitive to mass moods, whether the collective is experiencing fear, joy, grief, or hope. A Collective Empath might experience profound emotional shifts that seem unrelated to their personal life, often sensing the impact of global events, societal changes, or cultural shifts. This type of empath has an innate ability to sense the unspoken currents of humanity's collective experience, and they may feel compelled to contribute to healing, transformation, or support when collective trauma or unrest occurs.

While their heightened sensitivity allows them to be a source of compassion and guidance, they may also face challenges with emotional overwhelm, as the weight of collective energies can be intense and difficult to navigate without proper boundaries, grounding, transmuting abilities and rest.

Contrary Empath & Sacred Clown

Frequently, self-proclaimed Contrary Empaths call themselves "Heyoka" Empath. "Heyoka" belongs to the Dekota and Lakota peoples. One should only use this title for one's own if they have been accepted, invited, and named by their elders.

The Sacred Clowns are some of the rarest and most powerful of the empaths. They are revered as the most sacred of healers for many Native peoples and go by a variety of names. They are both sacred and profane as they have the ability to walk in all the worlds, commune with the elements, befriended by death and light, demons and the divine. They are born backward, spiritually gifted old souls in their youth, while also maintaining their childlike innocence. They tend to be feared equally as they are revered. They walk with energy that well exceeds the average person. Their lives are often riddled with hardships and opposition. They possess a variety of healing modalities, walk with most of, if not all the Claires and are multi-talented.

While there are a great many who are clown-like, they do not possess the gifts, initiation, sacrifice, native teachings, healing, and wisdoms. Instead, we call them, the jester, the fool and the contrary. This type of empath challenges conventional norms and mirrors the emotions of others, causing others to experience a change in perspective. They confuse those who observe them, as they have multi-dimensional experiences and expressions.

Cultural Empath

Cultural Empaths are sensitive to the emotions and energies of specific culture or society. They may feel deeply connected to traditions, rituals, or ways of life, often sensing the collective pain, joy, and history of those groups. These empaths may be drawn to specific cultural practices, often working to preserve or honor the wisdom of these cultures. Their work can be cumbersome as it involves recognizing and deconstructing deeply rooted generational trauma, ancestral healing, and the ability to bridge the divide.

Dream Empath

Dream Empaths are sensitive to dreams. They can interrupt dreams, prophecies, visions, and wisdom, and some even have the knowledge to visit others in their dreams. Dream Empaths readily experience astral travel and lucid dreaming. They may struggle with nightmares and lucid dreams that are not their own.

Earth / Geometric Empath

Earth / Geometric Empaths are in tune with changes to Earth's electromagnetic field, geometric abnormalities, and the weather. Some can predict patterns and occurrences. They can struggle with significant physical pain and illness during storms or times of mass distress in conjunction with multi-chemical sensitivities.

Emotional Empath

Emotional empaths feel the emotions of others on a deep level, in part by reading facial expressions and body language. They feel as though they have experienced the emotions of others. Therefore, they feel drained by others frequently. Emotional Empaths profoundly feel for their fellow humans and can have a challenging time in the presence of energy vampires.

Galactic / Solar Empaths

Like Earth Empaths, they sense the Schumann Resonance way before it is registered or at the same time. They can feel the energy bodies of the solar system and beyond, and some have a great inner knowledge of Astrology and Astronomy. Some will feel solar flares or other celestial activities as sensations in their chest or as heightened energies. Some may feel intense bliss while others can feel intense anxiety, anger, or exhaustion.

Historical Empath

Historical Empaths have the ability to connect deeply with the energies of the past. These individuals can sense and absorb the emotions, stories, and struggles tied to historical events or places. They may feel the weight of traumas or joy experienced by those who lived long ago, or they may experience vivid flashes of emotion and imagery associated with past eras. Whether visiting ancient sites, holding historical artifacts, or simply learning about specific periods in history. Historical Empaths often find themselves deeply moved or emotionally affected by the energies they encounter. This sensitivity allows them to act as conduits for understanding and healing the past, while also gaining wisdom from it.

Intuitive Healer Empath

Intuitive Healer Empaths are naturally gifted in the art of healing through energy and intuition. They possess the remarkable ability to sense where healing is needed within a person's body, heart, mind, and spirit. These individuals often intuitively "see" or "feel" energetic blockages, imbalances, or pain, enabling them to channel healing energy to restore harmony. Whether through hands-on healing, energy work, or simply being in the presence of someone who needs support, these empaths can help others find relief.

Physical Empath

Physical empaths can feel and interpret people's physical symptoms in their own bodies. Physical empaths can detect diseases and heal others, as they can transmute physical pain for others. Physical empaths may struggle with various physical sensitivities; however, they can heal themselves quickly.

Plant / Flora Empath

A plant empath senses the needs of plants around them. Plant empaths can communicate, feel, sense, and even see the energies of the plant world. These empaths are naturally gifted herbalists and are naturally talented in plant wisdom. Much like Earth empaths in that, they can struggle with food and multiple chemical sensitivities.

Precognitive Empath

Precognitive Empaths can sense the future. They may see future events in their dreams or feel them through heightened emotions or premonitions. Like the Intuitive Empath, they can keep those around them safe. These individuals may experience higher than average Deja Vu phenomena, or time distortions and disruptions.

Psychic/ Medium Empath

Psychic Empaths or Mediums, intuitively understand spirits outside of themselves. Psychic Empaths can communicate with beings and energies in other dimensions, including the spirits of people who crossed over. These individuals may struggle with headaches and other sensory discomforts.

Psychometric Empath

Psychometric Empaths sense the emotions and energy from objects. They may be able to relate things to specific people, locations, or events. They can be sensitive to buildings, land, and nonhuman energies.

Sexual Empath

Sexual Empaths possess a heightened sensitivity to sexual energies, both their own and those of others. These individuals can pick up on the emotional and physical states of those they are intimate with, or even those in close proximity. This deep sensitivity allows them to connect on a profound level with others, but it can also make them vulnerable to absorbing energies that are not their own. For these empaths, maintaining healthy boundaries is key to ensuring that they do not become overwhelmed by the sexual energy of those around them.

Sigma Empath

Sigma Empaths are a blend of highly intelligent sigma personality type and an empath. They are deeply intuitive and have a vast internal world. They tend to forge their own path, going against the grain of society, sometimes known as lone wolves. They are extraordinarily self-sufficient and prefer their autonomy and freedom. Like many empaths, they may feel taxed and overwhelmed by the demands of the outside world. However, when they do choose to make space for those in their life, they are solid and very loyal individuals. They require a lot of space because their sovereignty is of the utmost importance. They tend to value their solitude over societal demands.

Sonic Empath

Sonic Empaths are highly attuned to sound frequencies and vibrations, feeling the energetic impact of sound waves on both their own body and the world around them. Clairaudience is their most potent spiritual gift. This sensitivity extends to music, voice tones, environmental noises, the sounds of nature and electronics. Sonic Empaths experience physical or emotional reactions to sounds, such as a heightened sense of calm or, conversely, anxiety or discomfort. These individuals are often able to use sound for healing purposes, whether through music, sound therapy, or their ability to align with specific frequencies that promote balance and healing.

Telepathic Empath

Telepathic Empaths have a special connection that allows them to communicate and read others via thoughts and dreams. Often, their gifts are more apparent with those they are close to; however, some can tap into each other worldwide. These individuals can struggle with headaches and intrusive thoughts of others.

Tech Empath

Tech Empaths are sensitive to the energetic vibrations of technology, electronic devices, and even artificial intelligence. These individuals can sense when technology is "off," carrying negative energy, or when a device or environment is energetically out of balance. They may feel discomfort, anxiety, or a sense of being drained when using technology or being in tech-heavy spaces like offices, data centers, or areas with heavy Wi-Fi signals. Tech Empaths can also affect electrical components, such as lights or radio stations, due to their ability to influence the energetic field around them.

Quantum Empath

Quantum Empaths have an extraordinary connection to the quantum field and are able to sense and tap into the subtle energetic vibrations of reality. They are often able to perceive the interconnectedness of all things and can intuitively sense the shifting energies of time, space, and consciousness. These empaths may experience a sense of oneness with the universe and have a deep understanding of the multi-dimensional nature of reality. They can sense changes in timelines, realities, or dimensions and may have a profound ability to alter the energy around them, which can make them powerful healers and manifesters.

Chapter 7: The Spiritual Body

"Extension" ©*Zoila Luz Rosario Masiak 2025*

Everything is energy, and it is through frequencies and synchronicities that we discover the *Language of God*. You have a physical body; however, the spiritual body is where most of the energetic exchange happens. Your spiritual body is multi-facetted and multi-dimensional, and it is only in recent history that we have developed the ability to measure its effects. Your spiritual body is your light body, and it is layered with memories from your emotional body, mental body, physical body, consciousness, subconscious, thoughts, *dis-eases,* trauma, your past, past lives, ancestral memory, and epigenetics.

The spiritual body has an aura that you can see and perceive. Its extension far exceeds your ability to see it entirely, though you can observe its effects on others. Your light body envelopes all that is you, it is made of billions of energetic strings, like that of hair, each receiving and interpreting the information from your internal and external world.

Your Light body also has an electromagnetic field just like atoms and our Earth Mother. It is your nervous system that regulates your energetic body as well as your emotional body. Emotions are your energy in motion. Like a blade of grass, there is a taking in, and pushing out of energy. There is a constant flow into and through your body, and it must be expressed outward. It is through breath your spirit travels. Your throat chakra is your voice, your truth and your root chakra that houses your creation energy.

It is through the Light body that reiki healers, energy healers, and shamanic practitioners do their most diligent work. They are surgeons of the divine, patiently untangling the web of stuck energies in your body. You can do much of this work yourself simply by staying on top of good spiritual hygiene and focusing your light on the parts of the body that are screaming for attention. You do not need mind altering substances or retreats to do this work for yourself. Though there are times you may need assistance from outside yourself, as we cannot fully observe all that we are. Sometimes we need those outside observers to see what we cannot. The same is a true for the Creator and Source. It needs clear mirrors to reflect back to confirm its existence. Even the light is blinded by its own light.

The Spectrum of Energy Exchange

The spectrum of energy and its exchange is genuinely infinite. As a child, I came to understand this in my *be-ing* by playing with a prism, that my father had given me a from a telescope he had taken apart. I was mesmerized by the multi-faceted and multi-dimensional aspect of light. This was the moment I discovered; that I too was like a crystal, multi-faceted, multi-dimensional, and multi-talented. When looking at the Sun through the prism, the kaleidoscope of colors and grays produced a cascade of rainbows within rainbows, reflections within reflections, and some shades brighter than others. Still, no rainbow or facet is of one shape or color. The spectrum is as vast as the *Fractal of Life.*

Every being and entity will have multi-dimensional aspects, consciousness, experiences, and expressions, as proven by the laws of nature. To be a *hue-man* is to experience and emit different frequencies of light. Depending on your current state of *be-ing*, these frequencies are fluid and will fluctuate. Try not to let yourself get trapped in the high vibrational mindset. It is unrealistic to stay there, as the coming and goings of our experience change often. Your body must also integrate, rest and recover. It will take a toll if you have expectations that far exceed your vessel's ability to produce. Rest is just as revolutionary as empathy. creation and bliss.

Everything operates off energy exchange, and equivalent exchange is the most potent, as its potential to uplift becomes exponential. All vessels and energies (human and non-human) have the potential to grab attention and energy. It is not inherently a bad thing. It is how all beings evolved; it is also how we de-evolve.

The spectrum range contains all *be-ings*, entities and energies: from those who cause joy- to minor disruptions - to those who enjoy the chaos they generate- to those with more disturbing behaviors that devour the essence of others with ease - to those who prey and perpetrate sexual and physical harm to the most vulnerable part of the whole –*the innocent.*

Emotions are Energy in Motion

Like any form of energy, it can become too unstable for the body if not adequately cared for. Emotional intelligence begins to take on a whole other meaning when you deconstruct those energies and their effects on the four bodies.

Children are a prime example of such movement. Children move these energies out of their body with ease. They create, cry, dance, and play with little effort. They experience imagination and the *Eternal Now.* Their innocence and sweetness can light up any room, so long as you give them room to be. They generally do so with ease, and this is why children tend to be our wisest teachers, critics, and unfortunately prey to predators.

Your energy and time are the most valuable currency you will ever possess. As there is only one of you and your time here is brief. – *Your emotions are energy in motion.*

Learning to walk in ceremony and treat your vessel like the sacred divine *be-ing* that it is, will strengthen your discernment. If you feel more *dis-ease* than your heart sings, you are where you should not be. Do yourself a favor, and do not stay where your soul does not thrive.

They Know Not What They Do

Most people are simply unaware that they are projecting and sending attacks, while others are very much aware. Very often there is a lack of self-awareness and mindfulness, stemming from their own personal hell. It is vital that you know thyself and learn to maintain your spiritual body.

The Spirit of Apathy is very dense around those who are aware and do not care. Familiar situations hurt the deepest because they are the ones we hold closest. It is especially important that you learn to ground, stay on top of spiritual hygiene, and hold energetic boundaries so you are not swayed from your footing and connection to your Higher Self and Source.

Projections can induce emotional, mental, and/or spiritual instability if you are to believe another's view as your truth. Causing you to question your very own existence, mind, body, and soul, as well as literal nightmares in your dream state and your actual world. The most potent of the energy vampires can cause nightmares in both worlds.

Chronic exposure to trauma and energy vampires will also lead to emotional, mental, spiritual, and physical distress. The list of diseases that accompany excessive amounts of trauma is undaunting. Your body will give you information if you stop to listen. Knowing how different energies feel in your body is vital, to know what is of you and what is not of you.

The demands of holding your breath to mask will result in autoimmune attacks, chronic pain, chronic fatigue, severe joint pain, muscle pain, gastric disturbance, hives, hypertension, clenched jaw, heart pain, and mental instability. The layer of diseases will stack upon one another, until all organs are affected and disrupted.

Chapter 8: Spiritual Warfare

" The Timeless Battle of the Wills" ©*Zoila Luz Rosario Masiak*

Just like our spiritual bodies, spiritual warfare is multi-dimensional as well. The energies of your physical world and spiritual realms will be affected. It is a metaphorical and literal struggle against forces that aim to disrupt your connection to your peace, dreams, creations, harmony, Higher-Self and Source.

Spiritual Warfare is akin to psychological warfare aka "psyops." The purpose of psyops is to insight confusion and fear, making you easier to control and manipulate. The extreme versions will disrupt the psyche to the point of absolute collapse. Moments that steal your breath, energy, time, and focus, and disconnect you from your higher self has the potential to affect you and cause soul loss.

Situations that steal your breath away will have the most significant impact. When you experience a great divide, also known as soul loss, your vessel becomes open to *dis-eases* trickster spirits and parasitic attacks.

Service to Self vs. Service to Others

Service to Self vs. Service to Others. Cain vs. Abel. Creator vs. Destroyer. Dreams vs. Nightmares. Empaths vs. Narcissist. Helper Spirits vs Trickster Spirits. Light vs. Dark. Sovereignty vs Authoritarianism. Werewolves vs. Vampires. Windigokan vs Wendigo.

The timeless battle between apathy and empathy, duality of all that exists and which consumes it, the *War of the Minds and the Battle of the Wills*. Such legends and stories have rippled through the ages.

Service to Source vs. Service to Self, warning us of the unchecked powers of extreme individualism and a lack of accountability and respect.

Service to Others guided by Empathy aids in the potential to uplift and ripple outward exponentially much like the butterfly effect. It is in the knowing of anothers needs and the ability to hold space that nourishes and uplifts. It allows you to be the embodiment of Grace, offering unconditional love without judgment. This enables us to bless others, becoming the walking embodiment of miracles. You may never know why you blew into another's world, whether to aid, to learn from, to inspire or to teach. No act is too small when done with intent, heart, need, and a want for such miracles to happen.

The Return of Christ is synonymous with the rise in the Collective Consciousness and the Return of Empathy, — *The Great Mass Awakening.* For it was Empathy that Christ had been trying to teach the masses. It is far easier to teach a child about their empathy, their senses, their gifts, their energies, self-awareness, consciousness, and light body than it is through learning from suffering. We were never meant to burn. This *hue-man* experience is the vacation from eternity. It is in the great forgetting that forces us to dim our light, and in the awakening process and the return to self, a return to innocence, that we remember the kingdom of heaven is within. There is no other existence accept the experiences of any given moment.

You are indeed the gift to another and to our Earth Mother. Today, your light is needed more than ever. To dream the solutions, you cannot be chained by apathy, their nightmares, and the generational curses of the past.

Energies and Entities

What is in a name? A name is merely a mask or title for the vessel that contains the energies, emotions, entity, or spirit. Words hold identity, concepts, emotions, and imagery. Knowing all things contain energy and the ability to identify gives the ability to deconstruct, observe, understand, knowledge and wisdom.

Anything and everything can evoke emotions and feelings. Emotions are *energy in motion*. Everyone exchanges energy in some form or fashion. The key is understanding it; so that you do not waste your essence, your breath, your birthright, and your gifts. Those gifts become tools for a life filled with fewer *dis-eases*, the ability to heal and transmute for yourself and those outside of you.

Deconstruction and identification begin the first steps to unraveling the web of nightmares created by apathy and energy vampires. As you identify, you widen your scope of observations and understanding. Identifying energies and entities starts the process of breaking the spells that keep the energy from flowing freely.

All things have a multi-dimensional aspect. You can narrow the understanding down to two basic spirits, the Helper Spirits, and the Trickster Spirits. Though they genuinely encapsulate a wide variety of multi-dimensional aspects, and energies, and go by a variety of names.

Helper Spirits vs Trickster Spirits

Helper spirits guide, protect, and share wisdom but must be invited and shown gratitude. Helper spirits are the elements, nature, angels, ancestors, spirit guides, family, friends and anything else that offers you grace, protection, and wisdom. While your helper spirits are always there, you must invite them in. They are bound by the same laws of the Creator, as they cannot force, take hold and manipulate your *Free Will.*

Trickster spirits are very intrusive and do not care for your spirit or vessel. Trickster spirits are the ones that will trip you when you are not entirely in your body, causing accidents and giving way to parasitic attacks and shadows that will latch onto your emotional and mental states, they will keep you drained and stuck, hindering you from your path and purpose.

Parasitic energies are a little more dubious, as they latch onto your whole body. Such as fear and rage. Those states of being will render you lost to madness, and you are very easily controlled and manipulated in such a state. Divine Rage is quite opposite it is focused and very potent, as it has the ability to be harnessed, aimed, and applied to a particular target that brings about balance and justice to a situation. The epic battles of the Arch Angels often speak of such potencies.

Non-human entities

Non-human entities are buildings, concepts, elements, media, electrical, egregore, sounds, institutions, objects, places, planets, and everything in between.

More dangerous non-human entities that engage and perpetrate apathy are: Abuse of power of any kind, addiction, ableism, agriculture, assibilation, colonization, capitalism, consumerism, corporations, dogma, domestication, entitlement, eugenics, hording, human trafficking, infrastructures, genocide, governments, educational, financial, medical, and military institutions, all forms of media, resource demanding, lateral violence, mining, narcissism, spiritual narcissism, racism, patriarchy, pedophilia, white fragility, white supremacy, slave labor, and more.

Those who abuse, dismiss, or devalue the truths of others and the inherent sovereignty of life are a version of Apathy. – *The multi-masked foe and common enemy to us all.*

Egregore

An egregore is born from the convergence of collective thought, an energetic entity that thrives on the emotions, beliefs, and intentions of those who fuel it. Invisible yet profoundly influential, shaping perceptions and guiding actions in both subtle and overt ways. It feeds on the resonance of its creators, evolving as their consciousness shifts — growing stronger through devotion or weakening in neglect.

Some egregores inspire unity, wisdom, and divine embodiment, serving as celestial beacons of higher purpose, like that of Christ Consciousness. While others become parasitic forces, perpetuating cycles of control, fear, or apathy. Whether through sacred rituals, ideologies, or institutions, these entities whisper in the minds of those attuned to them, binding individuals to a shared energetic current that transcends time and space.

111

An egregore, no matter how ancient or deeply rooted, is only as powerful as the energy it is fed. To dismantle one, you must first withdraw your attention, refusing to engage in its illusions or rituals that keep it alive. These entities thrive on belief and devotion. Santa and the Easter Bunny are versions of egregores as they are concepts generally collectively agreed upon. Just as is Christ versus the anti-Christ. It is essential to expose the false narratives. The key to dissolving an egregore is not to fight it, for resistance only feeds it, but to starve it of its dominion over your consciousness. – *Unraveling the veil that clouds your sight.*

From there you must maintain a clear and sober mind. Once you clear your vessels of these energies, you may feel their densities from time to time. It is important not to let these energies bind you to the point of rigidity. Cutting cords, purging when necessary, transmuting, maintaining good spiritual hydyne and rituals will become as vital as bathing and drinking water.

Symptoms of Spiritual Attacks

When you experience a spiritual attack, your entire body reacts as if an internal fire alarm that has been triggered. All your senses become heighten, warning you of an energetic disturbance. A sudden wave of ickiness or an unshakable feeling of sliminess may wash over you, as though an unseen force is trying to cling to your energy field. You might feel hair standing on end, a prickly sensation crawling over your skin, nausea, or sharp cramps that seem to have no physical cause. Tension grips your neck and back, as if unseen hands are pressing down, and temperature fluctuations — burning hot one moment, freezing the next — can take over, signaling an energy shift. In some cases, the throat tightens, making it difficult to vocalize or call for help, as if something is suppressing your ability to speak. This overwhelming discomfort is not just a random occurrence; it is your body's way of sounding the alarm against external energetic forces, urging you that you in the presence of mal intention, you are not where you belong, and to cleanse, ground, purge, and transmute before the heaviness settles in. Make sure you are doing your due diligence to scan all four bodies. Make sure you have ruled out all other health concerns, as some of these symptoms can also be related to more serious health issues.

Accident Prone

> You will have more than average accidents and mishaps. You may feel you are unlucky at best. This is a sign that your spirit is not entirely in your body.

Autoimmune

> Weakened immune system. You are more prone to colds and flus. They will also take longer to heal from. This is caused by inflammation of your emotional and mental states that affect your physical and spiritual states. Unresolved grief and rage will express themselves in storms of hives, and they will last longer than need be if you are not calm, cool, and collected. In these moments, you are quite literally burning from the inside out.

Back & Neck

> Betrayal is felt between the shoulder blades, neck, head, and gut, like daggers, knives, and swords. Lower back and kidney pain may accompany. Betrayal will also affect your throat, heart, solar plexus, and sacral chakras.

Blood Pressure

Your blood pressure will rise when you are stressed, or it can drop. Most recognizable is high blood pressure or fluttering of your heart rate. However blood pressure disturbance of any kind will affect all your organs.

Burning

Evil Eyes will cause burning or prickly feeling to the whole body, but mainly to the back, primarily it is done when those who cast spells believe you are not looking. The dark heat from their eyes can cause nausea, burning in your back, and sometimes headaches and migraines.

Emotional Outburst

You will be prone to breaking down. You will be spooked or startled easily. Excessively tearful, defensive, fearful, or argumentative. It doesn't take much for you to get spun up. You must be mindful of who is pulling these energetic strings, because you are very easily controlled and provoked to hysteria and madness in this state.

Disorganized State of Mind

This will affect all manner of your internal and external world. It will show up in all that you do. The inability to hold focus and present will be more apparent. Those with anxiety and ADHD will see an increase in symptoms.

Disregard for Safety

Those who call you to disregard your safety usually have no regard for your precious life. These are the tricksters and energy vampires we must not play with, as they will readily induce nightmares of their own making.

Disregard for Your Vessel

Personal care and hygiene will take a back seat. You will not honor your vessel and finding the will to do so may seem impossible. You must honor your vessel. For you are a sacred Child of the Divine. Honoring yourself is akin to honoring the divine and the gift of life. This will also aid you in the ability to stay in the present moment.

Facial Droop

Over time, you will lose symmetry in your face. One side will droop, and it will become more apparent over time.

Financial Disturbances

You will struggle with money. In part because you are in fight or flight mode. This mode keeps you in a state of survival and it leaves little room to pay attention to your financial needs and to prepare for the future.

Your circumstances does not mean you are a failure as person nor does it define you. Our modern system teach us all, that poverty is your own failure or karma, despite its structure or the state of your health, social or economic status at birth. The system is parasitic by design, to extort your essence and time, and it places the blame squarely on your shoulders while accepting

115

none of the responsibilities for the poor design or lack of community.

Flutter

Bliss, death, and grief are felt deep in the heart, causing it to flutter and a sharp stabbing sensation.

Fog

Brain fog, dissociation, and time perception disturbances. Sometimes, the drain is so intense that sleep is induced, and your overall memory, and sense of self identity is affected.

Gastric

Poor eating habits or disruption in eating habits. It can be under-eating or even encouraging overeating, resulting in a wide variety of diseases, gastric distress, and malnutrition.

Purging may come through the release of distress, gas, laughter, sneezing, tears, or any bodily action that has an outward expression of relief of pressure.

Cruelty, disrespect, and misery to the Spirit may come through gagging or vomit inducing. It will smell foul, like a GI bleed, fish, marsh, or rot.

Headaches

False truths and illusions will give you a headache and make your eyes burn, as you must focus on being a part of another's world.

There may be intrusive thoughts (negative voices from those who spoke poorly towards you) that are clearly not yours. These are trickster spirits. You can tell the difference by the ability to change and redirect your thoughts. It will apply to actual events you've experienced if it is yours. If it is not, it will be vague and distracting, much like a mosquito in your ear.

Loss of sound, a feeling of swelling pressure in the top of head and the third eye tend to be messages. If it is from the helper spirits, there are solutions and a sense of calmness and clarity

If it is someone attempting to attack your psyche, or a trickster spirit a sense of panic starts to creep in. Perceptions and false truths that are not your own will be the biggest clue.

Hearing

Ringing in the ear can be whispers from your helper spirits or the ringing in the ear can be an intentional distraction. It is necessary to pay close attention to distinguish what you are and what you are not, what is for your highest good or what is stealing from you.

Hormonal Disturbances

You will have all manner of hormonal issues. The most noticeable will be high cortisol. Cortisol is your stress hormone.

Inability to Create

When you are being attacked, you tend to reside in a state of survival, it will drain you from your time and ability to imagine and create. This can cause a lot of mental anguish especially for artist, creators and dreamers.

Kidney

Kidneys process the toxins; this also applies to energy. Whether its food, substance abuse or excess levels of metals, fat, sugars, or cortisol. Your kidneys will be put to the test. Kidney stones, frequent UTIs, or kidney disease. This will manifest in lower back pain.

Lethargy

Feeling depleted when in their presence, even if it is many days, weeks, or months later. There tends to be an all-over malaise when space is shared. Such as an upset stomach, burning in the core, neck, back, anxiousness, and unease. Calling you to question your own sanity because it is not overtly violent or threatening.

Mental Disturbances

Various emotional, mental, and personality disorders: OCD, addictions, anxiety, brain damage, BPD, dissociations, eating disorders, suicidal ideations, PTSD, CPTSD and more

Dysregulated Nervous System

Spiritual attacks will dysregulate your nervous system. A dysregulated nervous system affects every part of your vessel. Anxiety, avoidance, brain fog, breathing issues, chronic fatigue, chronic pain, cardiovascular disease, digestive problems, depression, difficulty making decisions, dizziness or vertigo, dissociation, emotional numbing, fight-or-flight response, frequent illness, gastrointestinal disorders, heart palpitations, headaches or migraines, cold hands or feet, hyperactivity or restlessness, hypervigilance, increased sensitivity, irritability, intrusive thoughts, memory issues, mood swings, muscle tension, overeat or undereating, overwhelm, pressure response, rest-and-digest dysfunction, shaking or tremors, sleep disturbances, social withdrawal, substance abuse, tinnitus, CPTSD, PTSD, and autoimmune conditions.

Nightmares

Nightmares will disrupt your ability to flow with ease and create effortlessly. Nightmares and night terrors can be debilitating. Sometimes they will have a physical sensation as well, such as waking up in cold sweats or in a panic. Remember, whatever you are experiencing, it cannot hurt you unless you let it. Learning to control your dreams will help you through this.

Pain

Pain and pleasure can have similar sensations, such as a tickle. You can tell the difference by the feelings that arise. Learning to sit still in your vessel will aid in your ability to identify.

Pelvis

While breath is how your essence travels, so is your sexual energy, and it is the densest form of your essence. The root chakra holds a lot of energy, as it is your creation energy. Both in your artists manner and you bring life into this world.

Blockages in your ability to create as well as sexual trauma will be stored in this region. In the front of the pelvis, where the bladder and womb sit, you will find that the ancestral wounds of the mother are stored here. As women, we are the portals for life itself. In the back side of the pelvis, this is where you will find the ancestral wounds of the father.

The wounds of the past are not necessarily sexual in nature, though the feeling of being confined and blocked from the horrors of the past may be felt as stiffness. These are stored energies not of your own making, but it is vital that you move out. Dancing is one of the best ways to move these energies out, as it allows for flow, connection, grounding, purging, creation, and bliss all at once.

Rage

Rage, fear, mistruths, unspoken truths, and injustice, will make all your chakras feel blocked. Your heart, throat, solar plexus, and sacral chakras will be most notable. It can result in hives, all-over stiffness in the muscle, hot burning in the heart, gut, and rigidity in thought, joints, and muscles.

Reactive abuse

Like rage, reactive abuse, will be felt in the heart, throat, solar plexus, and sacral chakras. It will feel like a kick to the stomach, tightening of the feet, and clenching of the jaw.

Rigidity

The extremes of what I like to call the *"can't-want-to's"* make us beyond rigid in every sense of the word. Anxiety, despair, and fear will make your muscles burn, locking them in a place where you cannot move. When you are in this state, all chakras are blocked. Energy is not flowing freely as it should and in this way, you are in your own personal hell with little sight, as the smoke and fog is very dense.

Stolen Voice

Your throat chakra will feel blocked. You will find it hard to speak your truths. Your throat will feel very dense, blocked, and scratchy. Sometimes you will find that you are completely mute and when you do speak, little comes out and if it does, it feels forced or horse. What should feel effortless will require a lot of strength. Like any muscle, you must practice using it.

Temperature Changes

Anger, humiliation, and lust are felt as cramping, heat, or pains in the pelvis, chest, neck, and face. They are bitter and sharp to the senses.

While in the presence of energy vampires who deny your existence; the air may feel frigid to the bone, or the room may be excessively hot if there is agitation. Excessive heat or burning in the air from energy vampires who are feeling triggered. There will be a flushed feeling, as panic creeps into the bones and muscles.

False perceptions, and untruths will burn with their words and touch. Even a handshake or a hug can burn from those who wish you ill or who hold a lot of indifference towards you.

Chapter 9: Energy Vampires

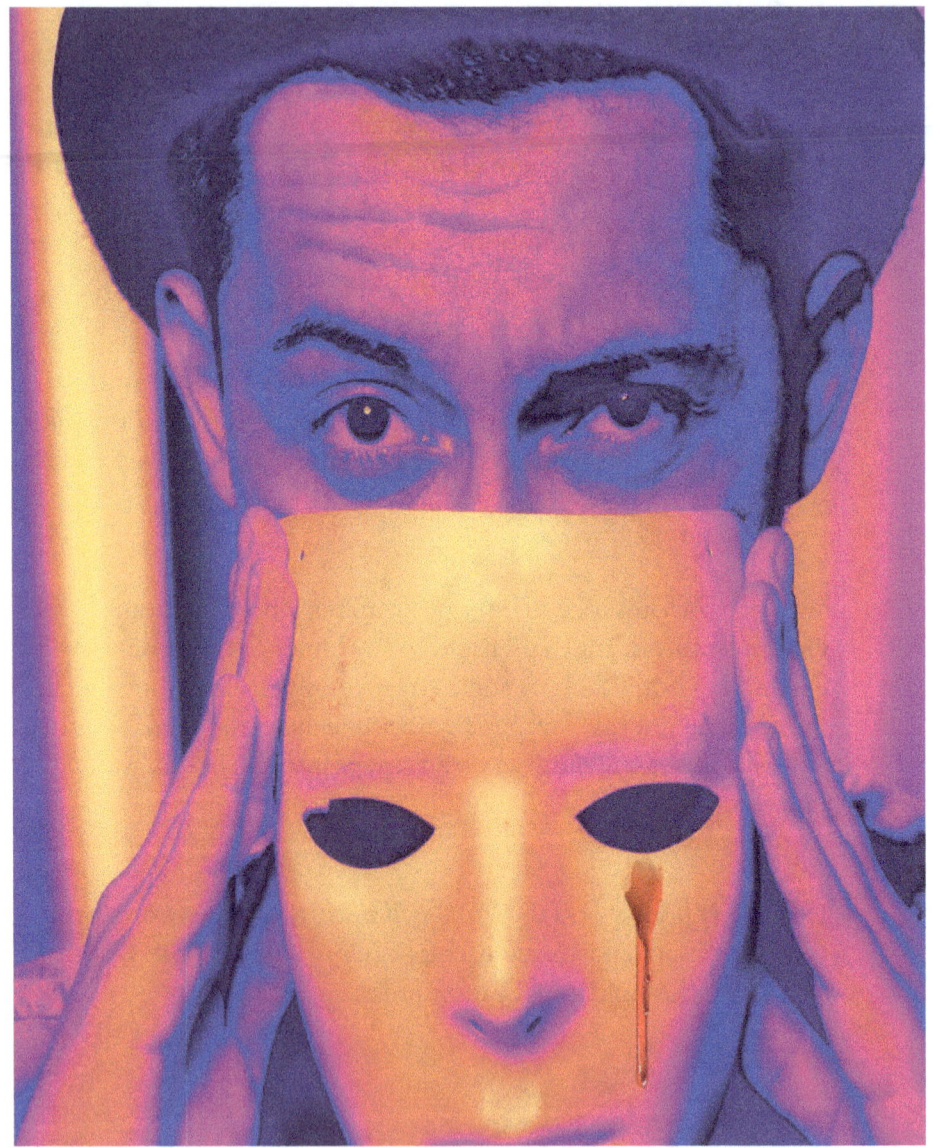

" Vampires" ©Zoila Luz Rosario Masiak 2023

The romanticization of Vampires has made the concept of having your essence stolen a rather lucrative and marketable ploy. Projecting into the minds of the masses, the glory of vampires. Their victims give up their power of choice, their Will Power, and essence freely. Most notably, you must invite them in, and if not willingly, then through coercion and manipulation.

Vampires require the *essence* in blood to survive–*human sacrifice*. Willing or unwilling, it makes no difference. Preferring the innocent and naive — those who have an abundance of light, are naturally sweet in nature, those who trust easily, and willing to step into their trap with little effort.

Unfortunately, due to self-domestication from the thousands of years of dogma, the knowledge that was supposed to be inherent to us all, has been the very chains that bound and suffocated the masses. Like any domesticated and caged animal subjugated and abused, the capacity for madness will sweep over the eyes, leaving the eyes dark, confused, and without light. It forces a very unnatural state of survival mode. All four of your bodies; emotional, mental, physical, and spiritual, cannot maintain homeostasis in such a state.

The systems and structures set in place forced so many into this state of being. There is no choice but to live confined. The devil is in the details, and they have structured all our lives down to the structure of seeds grown, modified, produced, and sold. There is little room for autonomy, liberty, or sovereignty when such suffocating systems exist.

Energy vampires wear many masks of gray, and the *Spirit of Apathy* is at the core of all that plagues them and this world; the Cannibal, the

Narcissist, the Skin Walker, the Trickster, the Wendigo, or the Zombie are all interchangeable. No matter what the name is, they are the multi-masked versions of *"The Evils of Apathy,"* the "me-me's," insatiable bottomless appetites, endless void, and hunger, as infinite as the variety of Life. The degree of damage correlates with the degree of separation from Source.

Apathy inherently oppresses life and aids the disconnection your Higher Self and Source. Life itself cannot be sustained under conditions of such rapid consumption. It is an absolute and quite literally and figuratively a disease of the body, mind, heart, and spirit with an infinite and insatiable hunger. It leaves only a wake of endless starvation and a halt to the existence of the life force as we know it. – *Apathy is the anthesis to Empathy, and Empathy is your direct connection to Source.*

The Name of The Game

"Name of THE Game" ©*Zoila Luz Rosario Masiak 2023*

The name of the game is called *Energy Monopoly*. Instead of playing with paper money, its currency is your breath, creative ability, energy, focus and time. All are finite while you reside in your vessel, making them the *most valuable* assets you will ever possess.

Our modern world has been designed to keep you disconnected. Those who participate in pedophilia and sexual abuse, genocide, resource hoarding, human trafficking, wealth and resource hoarding and war games are by far the most dangerous. Make no mistake, this is human sacrifice on a global scale. Money is meaningless to them. Your energy, however, now that is what they play with, that is what excites them, and that is what motivates them.

Energy in motion is your instinct; just like a chicken, it is your very essence. Your breath carries your spirit; it also aids in your vessel's fuel to sustain itself. The breath is by which the essence travels and your sexual energy is home to your creation energy. Your vessel is like a battery. The light comes into your *be-ing*, and then you express it outward. There is a near constant flow. Energy vampires distract and take your breath away, forcing you to hold your breath for extended periods of time, or through exhausting back and forth arguments with no results. This taking your breath away is where the exchange happens.

Energy vampires gain their strength by stripping others of their breath, creation, focus, and time. The loss of your breath will cause a loss of essence and potential soul loss. Frequent stolen moments can lead to a normalized state of panic and operating from a state of fear and survival. Prolonged periods without your breath will eventually lead to an arrest of said life. You cannot maintain homeostasis in such a state.

Energy exchange is a typical experience as that is the nature of being alive. Not participating in the games, not reacting, and remaining in your authentic energy, is what takes their breath away. It may upset them; however, it is essential not to let them know they hurt you. It will rob them of the power they are attempting to wield over you. You should absolutely speak up for yourself. However, if another is committed to not hearing you and purposefully misinterpreting you, then you are wasting your breath.

Simultaneously, empaths gain strength by taking the breath away from energy vampires; simply by not dancing with their nightmares and fully residing in your authenticity. This is done by staying in your body, fully present, being your authentic self and not responding. Your light will attract and act as a repellent. Your light will burn those who have not yet met their shadows, and many times, they cannot look you in the eyes.

When you believe lies, you are inherently betraying your own heart. Whenever you accept another's truths as your own, you will create pain in your body, further leading you off your path. Choosing who has your breath and refusing to let it be taken away without your agreement is a very potent tool.

Simply play opossum, by not engaging in the back and forth of emotional outbursts denies them their breath and the ability to maintain your strength in the most challenging situations. The satisfaction of seeing your spin in emotions is no longer in their control. No longer are you a toy for them to manipulate; instead, like an opossum that plays dead, you become boring, dull, less shiny, and no longer a source for their feeding needs.

What is an Energy Vampire?

Energy vampires are entities, environments, infrastructures, institutions, situations, structures, systems, and people who actively choose or passively disrupt and/or attempt to dim the light and drain others of their energy.

Most are oblivious and simply have poor habits due to those they mirrored and the masks they were forced to wear. Many are simply unaware due to growing up in a world that doesn't respect the breath and boundaries of others and certainly does not respect the most vulnerable and disenfranchised. Many times, energy vampires are unaware that they are attempting to siphon your energy. At best, they are indifferent to the exchange, allowing and contributing to unneeded confusion and illusions. Then there are those who actively seek others out to prey upon and are inclined to hurt children, disabled, elderly, women, and those they deem feeble or inferior. The most dangerous are the ones who know, don't care, and actively choose cruelty.

Energy vampires wear many masks, many tricks, have many shades of gray, and walk with many chosen acts of indifference. They tend to walk with a lot of spiritual parasites, such as: ableism, abuse, addictions, apathy, authoritarianism, colonization, disruptions, domestication, dogma, envy, entitlement, denial, gaslighting, greed, gluttonous, hoarding, narcissism, spiritual narcissism, pride, patriarchal ideals, false projection, sloth, wrath, white fragility, white supremacy, and more. There is a plethora of forms of energetic vampirism. Enough disruption in your psyche, and there will be an overall collapse in your body, heart, mind, and spirit.

How are Energy Vampires created?

Denying acknowledgment, eye contact, physical touch, speaking time, imagination, creations, dance, music, and play. These are the first worlds of an infant, the first experiences that imprint on the four bodies: emotional, mental, physical, and spiritual.

If betrayal and disconnection happen incredibly young, it creates a child who, from infancy, develops their all in survival mode. In that case, it will make for a heightened emotional state, higher than normal cortisol levels, and an overall increased risk for attachments, anxiety, addictions, delays, diseases, and sensitivities.

What do Energy Vampires feed off?

Energy Vampires feed off your breath, energy, essence, creation energy, time, and focus. Your breath is how your spirit travels through the ethers. Stifled or loss of breath will create moments of soul loss. These moments may cause blockages in your throat chakra, making it extremely hard for you to speak your truths. This is why your voice matters.

Your creation energy is stored in your root chakra, as well as your sense of security and survival, the foundation for the rest of your energy bodies, forward movement, and your divine sexual energy. This is how we are all born into this world, and it is a powerhouse for all that you create. Sexual energies require much respect, and you become powerful when you own your essence without influences from those who wish to siphon your energy. Your sexual energies are very potent, with the ability to create addictions, and on the other side, incredibly healing. Sexual energies can heal and improve the immune system, as well as dopamine, oxytocin, endorphin, serotonin, testosterone, prolactin, and creative abilities.

Frequently those who are attracted to you have no concern for your wellbeing. Unfortunately, after an encounter, your being will not be treated in a sacred manner you deserve, but rather as a toy for another person's use. After you are used up in their eyes, you will be treated poorly and discarded like a piece of trash. Some vampires may even become even more violent after intercourse.

Energy Vampires are excited by your essence, your Light, sweetness and the discomfort and fear they cause. They will attempt to diminish your joy, hope, love, light, excitement, or anything else that calls in the sense of bliss, flow, focus or justice. Like wild animals, energy vampires smell fear and become excited at your visible discomforts. If you react, they will attempt to feed more. Eventually needing more to fill those energetic needs. We must look no further than the historic vampires like Caligula and the Church. Prolonged periods of exposure to an energy vampire can make the mind question its surroundings and even call into question your very existence. Naivety, innocence, and sweetness catch and entangle many in their web of illusions.

What can you do?

Energy Vampires gain a lot of strength by dominating the airtime, attention, and focus. All of which keeps you distracted and disconnected from your Higher Self and Source. Energy vampires cannot handle being ignored and not heard. Simply walking away or not responding in the slightest; you will strip them of their power they are attempting to wield over you. It will create enough space that they will simply move out of your way. There is always a time and place when you must make your voice heard. However, not every situation must be a battle ground. You will lose energy, focus, and time if you play with their nightmares. Do not waste your energy or time with anyone who does not respect your autonomy and sovereignty. Do not let social pressure or media fool you. Your energies are your own. You are not required to be anyone's entertainment or toy. You are not meant to be consumed and consumed alone.

Energy Vampires sometimes become frustrated with you when they are being ignored. Ignore them anyways and keep it moving, listening to intentional music. It will drown out some, if not most, the static they are trying to cause. We are raised to be polite, but often in public, energy vampires will take advantage of these societal norms and expectations. If you can, do not engage. Do *NOT* react. This will strip them of the power they are trying to wield over you. Study their attributes so that you may side-step their chaos. You must also develop, learn, and maintain good spiritual hygiene and grounding practices. Eat healthy, move your body, dance, create, get plenty of rest, and support your vessel to the best of your ability. After all, it is your responsibility to take care of your vessel and spirit.

Make sure you are well hydrated and do lots of cardio before you enter a space that holds a lot of vampiric energy. Learning to hold your breath or shallow breath in their presence will help you maintain your composure, lower your blood pressure, give you time to observe your surroundings and space to find your exit. Seek a healer who can help you clear out the dense energies and stay on top of your spiritual hygiene and grounding practices.

Outward Expressions

Energy Vampires have no color, gender, shape, or size and are not confined to human form alone. Buildings, concepts, institutions of any kind, corporations, dogma, media, almost anything can drain the four bodies of their potential energy.

If you pay close attention, energy vampires in human form will show you their parasites. So often they do speak truths by way of projection. However, there are some physical changes you can notice when they let their mask down especially when agitated; however, they do not have to be agitated to show you, their parasites.

This is about energy exchange. Many are not self-aware nor are they conscious of their energies. In this way, they will harvest and siphon without knowing what they are doing. The more dangerous ones are very aware of the pain that they cause and are excited by their chaos and nightmares they cause for others.

Ableism

Energy vampires regularly show sign of ableism and at its core, ablism holds eugenic ideals. Ableism perpetuates societal attitudes that devalue people with disabilities, reinforcing a cycle of discrimination, exclusion, stigmatization, inadequate care, isolation, neglect, and social and economic injustices.

It hinders the full inclusion and equality in society to those who are medically, physically, or mentally fragile. Ableism can take various forms, such as inaccessibility, stigmatization, denial of autonomy, and underestimation of the capabilities of people with disabilities.

AI & Bots

While the digital age has allowed for an unending flow of knowledge, there is a new stage of spiritual and psychological warfare. AI generated bots are deployed simply to distract, confuse, and argue. More often than not, AIs will have nearly perfect grammar and lack imagination and nuances. On the other side of the spectrum of communication, AIs will present to you a lot of conformation bias and tend to be overly agreeable.

Images while detailed will be smoother than traditional work. Texture, like skin will still be smoother than a photograph or a painting and the colors will be brighter than that of original works. The lighting is near perfect and the back ground images are blurred and missing details. Most notable, there is a lack of an energetic field around living beings.

Without proper grounding and use of discernment, AIs have the capacity to induce psychosis. AI technology are good tools, however, always employ your discernment, do not allow anything or anyone take you down the pea patch of distractions or nightmares, most certainly not online.

Adam & Eve Spirits

While Adam & Eve are taught to be the first. Look no further than patriarchy for such tales. For there is no life without a woman and we are all female until the cells differentiate, around

7 weeks of gestation. Women are the divine portals bringing Source Light into Creation. Creation into Life. Life into *be-ing*.

The Adam Spirit is materialistic, looking to the flesh, the material world and outward expressions only. Many times they coincide with *"me-me"* energies. They depend heavily on their female counter part to carry the workload and the emotional labor of not only herself, their children but also for himself. They tend to be materialistic and lack awareness for anything they cannot physically touch, see or hear. Despite education, social or economic standing, they often lack depth and claim superior logic.

Eve is quite similar in many of the same attributes. Eve centers her worthiness around men and their needs. Consequently, she tends to be plagued with the *"Pick-Me"* energies and in so, will sacrifice other women and children to fulfill her needs.

Addiction

Energy vampires readily have addictions, masks for their own unresolved burning. Sometimes their addiction is mind altering substances, food, sex or creating chaos, sometimes it is the suffering of others, and sometimes they are addicted to their own suffering. Anything that can be abused will cause a degree of soul loss. Even too much oxygen will disrupt homeostasis.

Alienation

Energy vampires will alienate their prey from their families or shared peers. There is less resistance to their feeding needs if their target has no support.

Altruistic Narcissism

Energy vampires can display altruistic narcissism. They will engage in seemingly selfless or altruistic behavior, but their underlying motivation is often self-serving. Seeking admiration, validation, or a sense of superiority through helping others, rather than genuine concern for the well-being of the population they are serving.

Many philanthropists, adoption and foster agencies, non-profit and missionary pursuits are involved with such actions. Unfortunately, some are also involved with sanctioned human trafficking, money laundering, wealth hoarding, and their "good deeds" are a shell or a mask for their miss deeds.

Animal Abuse

Animal abuse takes on many forms. It can show up as neglect, lack of food or water, leaving an animal caged too long, excessive breeding practices, taking a young away too soon, purposefully walking into the animal or kicking them away, poisoning, to outright torture or sexual abuse of an animal. There is a basic lack of boundaries, a lack of respect for space and for the sacredness of Life.

Apathy Spirit

One of the most noticeable attributes is the apathy and indifference they have towards those around them. Apathy in my mind is the most dangerous. Like the overuse of salt, it is sprinkled and spilled everywhere, and it has no regard for the homeostasis of life, choking the life out of all who come in contact. Apathy shows itself through its indifference. Energy vampires will actively choose to cause chaos and nightmares while you are already struggling. In fact, they are more prone to attacking you when you are vulnerable. This is a hard lessons to learn when you hold a lot of empathy and light.

Artificial Noise

Rapid lights, sounds, high pitch frequency, or loud abrupt sounds can also cause you to lose focus. Densely populate areas allow for very little in ways of silence and introspection. All artificial, digital, electrical, mechanical, artificial lights and even Wi-Fi noise have the potential to disconnect and disrupt your connection to Source.

Arrogance

Much like a rooster, energy vampires will show bold displays of arrogance. Arrogance is the illusion of superiority, a mask for insecurity and otherisms' which leads to separation. Where confidence is rooted in knowing oneself.

Assimilation

Energy vampires regularly depend on assimilation to hold dominance over society. They require a certain level of cohesion to maintain control. Boarding schools, public schools, medical, and military institutes are most notable.

Forced assimilation has included the imposition of dominant languages in schools, the outlawing of traditional practices, forced sterilization, and the relocation of communities. The consequences can be devastating, leading to the loss of languages and traditions, deep psychological trauma, and the erasure of ethnic culture and identity. Taking with it its knowledge, medicines, and wisdom.

Authoritarian

Energy vampires will express direct or passive frustrations when there is a perceived challenge to their "perceived authority." Actions and words are monitored and given little space to speak freely unless it agrees with their direct expectations or experiences. Using their power of authority or perceived authority to dim the light or stifle others. They dismiss, diminish, and talk over those around them, pretending others are non-existent, even in a shared space. This is to devalue, humiliate and maintain authority, dominance, and control.

Backhanded Honesty

If you pay close attention, they do expose themselves in the way they communicate. Such as confession of feeling jealous, wishing to harm others, by projecting or through "joking."

Energy vampires will use subtle or disguised criticisms that appear to be truthful but are designed to harm, manipulate, or undermine, often framed as "constructive feedback" to disguise hostile intentions.

Blame-Shifting

Energy vampires will deflect responsibility onto others to avoid accountability for their actions or behaviors. Followed by shifting the blame onto you or those who spoke up. Also known as DARVO, an acronym that stands for Deny, Attack, Reverse Victim and Offender. It is a psychological tactic used to deflect blame and responsibility by denying their wrongdoing, attacking the victim's credibility, and falsely portraying themselves as the victim. This tactic can be insidious and difficult to recognize.

Breadcrumbing

It is akin to leaving a trail of "breadcrumbs" to keep you following along without any real commitment. They will be very involved and overly invested then slowly sending occasional, non-committal messages or signals to keep someone interested without any intention of committing. It is used much like a lure; they will toy with your emotions and play in your face.

Child Abuse

Children produce a lot of light and energy. Energy vampires have a particular attraction and disdain for children. Abuse comes in all forms and often they coerce children to hide their assaulting behavior. Not all forms of abuse are visible.

Cat Fishing

Catfishing is when someone creates a fake online identity to deceive others or creates a false persona about themselves for dishonest reasons such as emotional manipulation or financial gain. Eventually, they drop the masks, as they cannot maintain them for prolonged periods. Usually, their actions will give them away.

Charm Offensive

While charm is quite the spiritual gift, energy vampires will use excessive charm or flattery to disarm or manipulate others into compliance or vulnerability.

Deflection

Energy vampires will avoid direct answers or accountability by redirecting conversations to unrelated topics or focusing on others' flaws. They will also use this tactic to minimize and devalue your efforts or accomplishments.

Cinderella Effect

Energy vampires will not help you maintain shared surroundings. In fact, they will create a lot of chaos and mess but will not help clean up. They will actively diminish, devalue and humiliate you in every conceivable way possible. Their lack of help is their way of maintaining control and keeping you busy rather than participating in shared spaces. They make demands and expectations that far exceed their own output. It is amazingly easy to toil your essence and time away cleaning behind others, so much so, you may not be aware that it is happening.

Energy Vampires tend to enjoy being served, especially from those they deem less than. Often times, they are distracting you from your own potential that they have already witnessed, they are just hoping you won't notice.

Collections, Hoarding, & Gotta-Collect-Them-All Spirits

Sometimes, energy vampires can acquire enormous collections. Their nests can be quite large. This could be people, places, or things. I like to call this the, *"I gotta collect-them-all"* energy, just like the dragons of old. There is little time for actual focus and intent to care for all the needs of their acquired treasures, paving the way for potential abuse and neglect.

With people collecting, there may be some care for the group, but they do not manage their exchange mutually. The group maintains that for them as well as their feeding needs. Constantly feeding off the energy they get from being the center of attention. Spiritual leaders who exhibit spiritual narcissism are prime examples of such collections. Vessels are seen as objects, not multi-dimensional, sovereign, self-actualizing, and fully governing spirits.

Colonized Mind & Colonization Spirits

Oftentimes, energy vampires have a colonizer mindset. The *"colonization spirit,"* prioritizes consumption, power, control, and dominance over others, exhibiting a sense of superiority and entitlement to the resources at hand. They believe or covertly act on the premise that they alone have the inherent right to impose their culture, values, and systems on those deemed inferior or primitive. This perspective fosters a *lack of empathy* for the colonized, justifying exploitation and oppression. They will deny basic human dignity and rights, such as food and water, and have an eye for exotics.

In contrast, a colonized mind internalizes the beliefs and values of the colonizer, leading to self-doubt and disconnection from their own heritage. The grapple with a fractured identity can be undaunting and cause for a lot of pain, internalized colorism, racism and misplaced anger and confusion.

Competition & Zero-Sum Thinking

Energy vampires will view you as direct competition, even if you are unaware of said competition. Their actions may be covert or in your face. They take a Zero-Sum Thinking approach.

Zero-sum thinking is the idea that in a situation, one person's gain is considered an equal loss for someone else. It assumes that resources or benefits are fixed, and any positive outcome for one person comes at the direct expense of others. This contrasts with the idea that cooperation and community can lead to situations where everyone involved can benefit, known as positive sum thinking.

Cognitive Dissonance

Many times, energy vampires cannot see their own shadows. They become very irritated at anything that disrupts what they deem normal. Such as ableism, racism, internalized racism, etc. Cognitive dissonance is a significant problem when individuals confront conflicting beliefs or behaviors, resulting in psychological discomfort and confusion. This can be a very deep problem for the abusers and the abused.

Conformity

There is an inherent need for conformity and for others to conform to their perceived ideals. Authenticity, empathy, imagination, creation, self-expression, and sovereignty are sometimes foreign to the authoritarian needs of an energy vampire. Frequently, these elementary ideals upset vampires the most.

Consumption of Energy

Energy vampires devour the essence of others with ease. The more dangerous ones have an insatiable sexual appetite. While they may not be actively participating in a bold display of consumption, lack of action is as damaging as the act itself.

Modern media has spent much of its time grooming children and normalized having your light and essence consumed. Consequently, many actively seek to be consumed, the need for attention predominates their safety and wellbeing. This can be very damaging to the psyche and development of a child and to society at large.

Denial

Energy vampires use denial either by way of gaslighting, or denying you space, food, water, resources, and anything is up for grabs. This is used to maintain dominance over a situation.

Destiny Swapping

Energy vampires will see the light and want it for themselves. It will be displayed as mimicking your actions, aspirations, ideas, words, and aesthetics. Simultaneously not giving you credit. They will monitor and hang on to what you are doing and sometimes will become quite close, praying on your interests and "similarities."

They will drain you of your energy, actively sabotage your efforts, and wish for your downfall. You can see these displays throughout the entertainment industry; where a friend or partner starts acting like the other, and one becomes drained, while the other who is mimicking gains. Stolen or denial of inheritance is another version of destiny swapping.

Devalue

Energy vampires will disregard and devalue the efforts made. They are unaware of the measures taken to create and produce something. The exchange of energy and time is always unequal and not reciprocated. They will actively compliment others and make a point to make sure they do not acknowledge your presence. Energy vampires will not add to the overall value of another person unless they benefit their motives. Inherently devaluing those who surround them.

One of the ways this is done is by purposefully not looking you in the eyes or pretending they do not see or hear you. They are fully aware of your presence; they are just attempting to stifle your light.

Dismissal

Energy vampires hold no value in what you hold close to your heart. They will downplay your experiences and other forms of ableism, microaggression, and lateral violence. They will dismiss and normalize the afflictions caused by their actions.

Distractions

Energy vampires will purposefully distract you from your work, avoid helping, and/ or even take credit for your efforts and time. Profiting in some form from the original creator. Intentional interruptions, long pauses, rapid, alerting speech, talking over, or switching subjects abruptly & rapidly. These acts to distract, take your focus, and energy and can take your breath away, forcing you to hold your breath for extended periods. This taking the breath, focus, and time away is where the exchange happens. Demanding, or the stalling of actions, results in loss of energy focus, time, and even the perception of time can be distorted.

Dogma

Dogma is a tool energy vampires use to maintain power and control over the masses. These ideals have a strict set of rules that do not allow for questioning as they tend to be rigid in thought and action. Anytime there is a restriction of discovering your vast internal world, higher self, and consciousness, and that of the external world interrupts your *Free Will. Free Will is the Muscle of Choice;* taking away choice inherently oppresses the Will of the Creator.

Domestication

Domestication is an ancient tool cultivated by energy vampires. It involves the process of taming and adapting wild animals or plants for human use. Many of your social norms are based in domestication rather than the homeostasis of the overall environment and personal autonomy. Domestication results in changes to the physical and behavioral traits, making you easier to control and manipulate.

Ego

Energy Vampires tend to move with their egos first. Their internal programming is set on automation, and many times they are not aware they are running from such a state. Like alcohol abuse, they can become drunk from their over inflated egos and the position of power they hold. Just like dealing with anyone who has an addiction, they can be very irrational creatures. Their egos become bruised easily, and they will overreact to perceived slights or when confronted.

The larger the ego, the more grandiose the reaction and posturing. Very often they are like toddlers in adult bodies. Yes, they can perform standard functions, but it does not extend past services to self. While the ego is an essential part of your *hue-man-ness* and it will aid you in all manner of ways, this is quite different for an energy vampire.

Elderly Abuse

Energy vampires will disregard neglect, manipulate, emotionally, mentally, and physically harm the elderly. Like children, the elderly require a lot of care and time and are unable to defend themselves. This is most unfortunate, because our elders are walking libraries of experiences and insights, which teach us to course correct or avoid problematic situations all together.

Energy

When you are in the presence of an energy vampire, their energy field becomes dark, dull, and spiky. Sometimes, their energy will feel slimy, and there may be a foul odor that is not overly apparent. This is not the same as perfume or body odor. It is the energy that surrounds them. Their presence alone can make your hair stand on end. They will affect all your senses even your body temperature will fluctuate depending on whether they are angered or dismissing you.

Entitlement & The Me-Me Spirits

Energy vampires have an overall perceived sense of entitlement to your breath, energy, emotions, focus and time. Some even feel threatened by your vessel's inability to handle such stresses. Walking with what I like to call the *"Me-Me's"* energies, aka bold displays of selfishness and unwillingness to compromise their comfort or preferences for others.

Entities & Parasites

Parasites are energetic or spiritual entities that feeds off a person's life force, emotions, or personal energy. They inherently cause confusion and disconnection. Energy vampires may walk with some or many. All their tactics are used to diminish and suppress your light.

Envy

Energy vampires may express the need to one-up. There can be great offense if the limelight is not on them. Envy arises from comparing yourself to others. This can involve social, economic, or personal aspects. Energy vampires seem to enjoy hating the light in others. Often, the bliss and joy in others are not trusted. Those who hold a lot of sweetness can be the most threatening to energy vampires, as they reflect all that an energy vampire is not. Energy vampires gain strength by diminishing the light of those they deem inferior.

Emotional & Mental Abuse

Energy vampires often use this form of abuse to maintain control and dominance. It will consist of verbal threats, insults, gaslighting, intimidation, humiliation, isolation, and other tactics that undermine a person's self-esteem, and psyche. Extreme exposure can create BPD, PTSD, CPTSD, cognitive dissonance, imposter syndrome, and can even call into question your very own existence.

Emotional Dumping

Unloading emotional burdens onto someone without their consent, often overwhelming or draining them. While there is nothing wrong with sharing, this is done in excessiveness and inherently lacks respect for another's personal space and energetic boundaries.

Evil Eye

The evil eye is another favorite tool energy vampires use. Used individually or to signal to others to join in to dim and silence, your light and voice. It calls in shame and unjust judgment and/or punishment of others. The sick energies hide behind the dark glares.

There is usually some upset from your presence. Mothers will do this to signal to a child that something is unsafe. However, energy vampires use this signal as a punishment and a tool for silence.

They may feel threatened by those who will look them in the eyes. They will intentionally avoid eye contact to dismiss and disempower those they have deemed less than or if they feel threatened by your authenticity and light. Or the extreme opposite, they attempt to stare you down until you sit down.

Eugenics

Energy vampires perpetuate the ideals of eugenics by the policy they put in place, through actions of indifference. Policies such as assimilation, dehumanizing efforts, unnecessarily cruel wide spread tactics, forced sterilizations, the promotion of racist and discriminatory policies, and genocide. It is a supremacist ideal, and it is upheld by those who believe others are inferior.

Exploitation of Empathy

Energy vampires will use your empathic kind nature against you to extract emotional labor, validation, or resources. They will also weaponize your empathy as a weakness or a character flaw.

Eyes

The eyes of energy vampires will grow dark and flat, taking on the appearance of looking black and hallow, especially if they do not see you as one of their own. Rather than looking at you, they will appear to be looking through you or as if you are an object. It may not always appear as rage, but there is an overall contempt for your existence.

Often referred to as demon eyes, dead eyes, siren eyes or shark eyes. Sometimes their pupils become very narrow or completely dilated, or the bottom of their eyes will show their whites, like they are looking upward but they are not.

They may appear conscious and awake, and they will act as if they are, but their eyes and body language are cold, lacking the luster of a fully conscious and sovereign *be-ing*.

Facial Expressions

Their grins are flat and forced. There is little movement in their facial expressions despite their words or tone. They also will snarl their nose or curl their lips. Their disdain will be noticeable, despite their attempts to hind behind their masks.

False Justification

Energy vampires will claim superior logic to their excuse for their apathy or violence. Making them prone to the justification for said action or lack of.

False Mirrors

Some energy vampires have the ability to mimic the light and charisma, but they cannot hold or maintain the light for long durations of time, nor can they produce it on their own, or at least not sustainably. The more vampiric in nature, the longer they can hold the form of those they are mirroring.

No matter how many filters or how much makeup, they lack a certain level of sparkle. Their auras are dim, dull, and unnecessarily spiky. Even walking into a room without words is enough to cause unease and an energy exchange. Even in silence, they will make you grapple for your breath.

With comfortability, their attached entities will flash. Darkness in their eyes and the whites show more. The eyes will appear dull and miss the shine of an awakened and sovereign *be-ing.*

Fear

Fear is one of the most successful tools energy vampires use to control. Fear has always been a powerful tool for those wishing to maintain control and power. Keeping you in a state of confusion, panic, and survival mode, is how they maintain control. Introducing different but the same nightmares when they see fit. They will corner, intimidate, or cause nervousness in those around them. Those who are the closest receive the heavier end of the rod.

Financial Abuse

Money is another form of currency for the exchange of energy, focus, and time. Though money itself is not inherently "bad" it is misused. The unfortunate truth is that our modern world values money over the sanctity of Life, and it is one of the more common types of abuse.

Energy vampires will use money as a means for control. This may result in refusing to aid in another's needs, controlling the financial situation of a home unit, or disinheritance. Energy vampires will use money as a means to hurt another or a situation, not always for their financial gain, but to manipulate and maintain control.

Gaslighting

Energy vampires have a tendency to use gaslighting to manipulate a situation. They will use confusing and distracting techniques that cause one to doubt everything and anything, even your own existence, may be vague to you. They will systematically deny you your own accounts and experiences.

Sometimes gaslighting is a knee jerk reaction to cognitive dissonance.

There is a lack of accountability, defensiveness, and/or lashing out when grievances are brought up. Routinely implying that the grievances brought up will always be your fault for "not understanding" their words. The attempts to communicate grievances are perceived as threatening. They will blame you for their reaction because you brought grievances to their feet.

Gluttonous

Energy vampires can be quite gluttonous either by way of food or extravagance. They either devour your resources, or they will parade all that they have while simultaneously denying you your basic needs and respect.

Grooming

Energy vampires readily take part in grooming behavior, normalizing the sexualization and exploitation of those around them, a serious cause of intergenerational trauma. Media of all kinds have worsened this problem, normalizing the misuse of children, weaponizing humor, and all manner of grand acts against humanity.

Grooming steals breath and innocence, and misuses of your sexual energies. Your sexual energy is one of your most sacred energies, as it is your creation energy. Grooming is not always sexual in nature; it also applies to cruelty and humiliation.

Gossip & Casting Shadows

Energy vampires will gossip, spread false truths, and convince others to think poorly of you. This is what we call, *"Casting Shadows."* They sow doubt in the minds of people, casting shadows over your image, making it harder for others to see you clearly. Support from a group offers them validation and vindication. The more vampiric in nature, the more psychological and social tactics they use to control their prey. Eventually needing more to fill those energetic needs.

Gang Stalking

As our social world has changed so has the nature of spiritual warfare. Energy vampires will use gang stalking; it can be very subtle to highly violent communication. It is a digital form of group manipulation. It is not always overly obvious; it can be outright bullying from a small group or a large group that can push someone to the edge. Like bullying at school, this is done via social media. Using your social media post against you and/or manipulating your words. It can come from people who know you directly, strangers, from fake accounts or reposter accounts (accounts that have no profile and only repost others' content) Sometimes you will find your content on these users' sites. These users will engage with said group, watch your content but not say a word to you directly.

Sometimes they can be very violent with their word choice, threatening or telling someone to kill themselves. Other times, they will create memes and/or posts, or a group chat that will share with you directly or covertly. Other times they will watch your content from the sidelines, not engage.

They will have a single person with whom they all engage with. That person will outright devalue and ignore you while boosting those who follow their lead. It can happen to children of school age all the way to adulthood. Often the only link the group has been a dislike or distrust of you. It is crucial that you do not react and block all users that you suspect. Sometimes you will need legal advice or for the courts to step in. In which case, screen record and screen shoot everything, and document the dates and times to the best of your ability.

Guilt & Shame

While feeling guilty or ashamed of a situation can be a proper response. These can be profound learning moments, and opportunities for growth. Rather than a tool to learn from for their own personal lessons, energy vampires will project onto those around them.

Energy vampires will use shame to emotionally and mentally manipulate a situation. This is not the same as sharing one's truth, this is repeated acts. They will project their guilt and shame onto those around them.

Homophobia

Everyone has their preferences; however, energy vampires take it a step further by directly and systematically engaging in harmful acts of those who identify as LGBTQ+. Some energy vampires have an irrational fear and misplaced anger, oftentimes an internal war that is expressed outward in harmful acts against those who do not conform to their standard of gender or sexual orientation.

Hostility

Energy vampires can be unreasonably hostile and angry. This can be seen in any situation as there is no respect for boundaries. There will be an overall disdain for your presence.

Human Sacrifice

Any time and in any situation, you trade in human bodies, and they are not sovereign, is a form of human trafficking and sacrifice. Even if you are married, and feel you are required to perform sexual duties for exchange for basic needs or financial relief, it is a form of trafficking and an exploitation of your vessel and essence.

More dangerous energy vampires are the ones who participate in these activities. Creating situation that lack basic dignity, livable wages, and generations of poverty. The use slave labor for agriculture, factories, mining, housework, sex slaves, torture, or war, etc. Make no mistake, this is human sacrifice on a grand scale.

Humiliation & Humiliation Rituals

Humor is good medicine. However, energy vampires misuse and weaponize humor and laughter; this is what we call a *"humiliation ritual."* As it is rarely employed once. Their humor is riddled with cruelty. Inciting humiliation within a private setting or in public. We are social creatures, and this form of punishment is overlooked and quite damaging to bystanders and the victim alike.

Energy vampires will purposely call attention to you publicly, whether by way of comments or intentionally taking distorted and unattractive pictures of you. They will purposefully ignore any request to stop. It could be through aggressive behavior or simply obnoxious behavior.

Public humiliation can be quite effective, as it calls in other energy vampires to enjoy and join in the parade. In this situation, everyone around them is subject to watching, thus becoming active participants and victims of cruelty at the same time.

Jealousy

Energy vampires may display tones of jealousy. Feelings of insecurity, fear, and resentment. It typically arises when a person perceives a threat to a valued relationship, by the way others treat you or your position. At its core, jealousy arises from feelings of inadequacy or fear of loss. When they feel threatened, it will amplify their insecurities, leading to destructive thoughts and behaviors. You will find envy and jealousy at the root of *"destiny swapping"* and violence.

Judgment

Judgment creates separation. It can come from numerous places like envy and jealousy to a superiority complex or the need to maintain control. Energy vampires will pick you apart and use judgment as a way to make you question your inner knowing and your light.

The Karen & The Kyle

Energy vampires who have an over inflated sense of entitlement, as I like to call them the *"me-me's."* They are quick to make a scene and have a need to maintain authority to get what they want. They are quite aggressive and demanding individuals who lack empathy, self-awareness, and self-control.

Lack of Boundaries

No space is sacred. All areas of shared space are up for grabs. This is energy monopoly, after all. This includes while in the bathroom, in the shower, or in moments when you are too ill to care for yourself. They deny and neglect the basic dignity, needs and respect of others. Actively seeking out situations in which you clearly gave a verbal, direct, and firm boundary that must not be crossed.

They will knowingly walk uncomfortably close to crossing that boundary. They do not respect the sensory needs of others, consequently forcing others to ignore their bodily autonomy. A simple example is forcing a child to eat something that makes them want to vomit or that hurts their stomach or withholding bathroom facilities or water.

Lateral Violence

Energy vampires use harmful and destructive behavior that occurs within a marginalized or oppressed group, directed at their own members rather than the oppressive external group. This results from the frustration and stress experienced by individuals within the marginalized group who may redirect their anger and pain toward one another instead of addressing the root causes of their oppression. It can take the form of bullying, *"casting shadows,"* humiliation, undermining, gossiping, shaming, or any behavior that perpetuates a cycle of oppression, creating conflict and division within the community itself.

Limited Imagination

Conversations with energy vampires are limited to entertainment, materialism, and other people, rather than actual ideas and concepts of their own. They share the same information and nightmares, but they offer no solutions created on their own, resulting in limiting beliefs.

Love-Bombing

While there are many who follow their hearts and are empathic and show their love effortlessly. Energy vampires weaponize the "acts" of love, overwhelming someone with excessive affection, attention, or praise to gain their trust or create dependency, often followed by withdrawal or manipulation. It is very unfortunate as unconditional love has the power to heal and uplift.

Lying & Sin of Omission

Energy vampires have an ability to lie without blinking an eye either by way of falsifying facts or through omission. The Sin of Omission does not necessarily mean they are doing a terrible thing; they are just not doing the right thing. For some, it takes a lot of courage to speak their truth. There is a plethora of reasons for their lying, anxiety of getting in trouble or because they purposefully want to cause harm. They can be habitual, even believing their own lies. The worst are quite proud of their ability to keep track and to *"weave"* stories. As always, it is to seek control and to manipulate a situation to their favor.

Matilda Effect

The Matilda Effect is seen throughout history. Where a woman's deeds are deemed null and void, and her male counterpart is given credit. This is a systematic erasure of the feminine, rooted in patriarchy and dominance. The tragic loss of Mary Magdalene wisdom is a prime example of such an effect. Without Mary's ability to perceive Christ fully, we would not know of his resurrection. Energy vampires of this nature are typically male or the benefactors.

Manipulation

Energy vampires regularly use manipulation. Manipulation involves influencing or controlling someone's thoughts, feelings, or behaviors, in a deceptive or unfair way. They will attempt to weaponize your empathy against you. Ultimately, the goal is to control the situation and the outcome.

Medical Abuse

Medical Abuse has a vast range of situations. It can happen at the hands of the staff, doctors, institutions, insurance companies, from the public or from family members. Energy vampires will create situations that will make you gravely ill or injured. They will either neglect, over medicate, refuse care, or cause physical and sexual harm. The elderly and the medically fragile are particularly vulnerable. Mother Teresa, while famed for her hospitals, is a prime example of the horrors that occur in medical institutions.

Masks

Energy vampires wear a wide variety of masks and will require you to do so as well. An authentic, empowered, and aware *be-ing* is often the one who has the ability to be the most threatening to an energy vampire and their nest. This is because the authentic light has the ability to shift energies in the room and often reveal what they are not. They lose the attention, energy, and focus of those they are trying to manipulate.

Micro Aggression

Energy vampires will use very subtle, everyday actions or comments that convey prejudiced, discriminatory, or derogatory messages toward individuals or groups based on their race, gender, ethnicity, sexual orientation, or other characteristics. Microaggressions can take various forms, including verbal, non-verbal, back handed jokes, minimizing comments and gestures, or passive aggressive behavior that contributes to a hostile and unwelcoming environment for those who experience them.

Micromanagement

Energy vampires will use micromanagement as a form of control. Micromanagement is a suffocating force that strips a person of their autonomy. It stifles intuition, creativity, and confidence, forcing you to second-guess every move, fearing mistakes more than they value growth. The weight of constant oversight breeds anxiety and resentment, leaving you exhausted.

Mimic the Light

They can mimic the light, but they cannot maintain it. The more vampiric the longer they can mask. Pay close attention to their actions and projections.

Monitoring & Fly Spirits

Energy vampires tend to monitor your actions and your speech. They keep tabs but offer no support. These are called *"fly spirits."* Simply put, you will never convince a fly that honey tastes sweeter than caca.

Narcissism

Energy vampires who walk with narcissism have a sense of entitlement, arrogance, lack empathy and a tendency to manipulate or belittle others to maintain their self-image.

Neglect

Energy vampires can be neglectful to their surroundings and to those around them. Their wants supersede the needs of others. It does not matter if requests are made or not. Basic dignity and necessities will be denied.

Nightmares, Chaos Spirits & Flying Monkeys

Energy vampires consciously or subconsciously create situations that will cause you to be sleep-deprived through acts of indifference, arguments, fear, violence or encouraging poor sleep patterns. If there is enough emotional upset before sleep, they are more likely to cause nightmares or overall unrest — long periods of unrest and turmoil will cause *dis-ease* and illness to set in.

Nice

Energy vampires will often mask their deceit with behaviors that seem *"nice."* To be nice refers to being pleasant and agreeable in behavior, focused on social etiquette and politeness. While kindness, on the other hand, implies a deeper level of empathy and compassion. Kindness involves genuine concern for others' well-being. Describing another as "*nice*" doesn't mean a person is good or kind.

Objectification

Energy vampires will see you as an object for their personal gain or as a toy to play with. There is little regard for your autonomy, vessel, and little sight for your spirit. Many times, believing they own you or that you are indebted to them.

Opportunist

Energy vampires will take advantage of situations, particularly for personal gain, without regard to principles or ethics. They will exploit circumstances for selfish or strategic reasons, often at the expense of others.

Passive-Aggression

Energy vampires will express negative feelings indirectly through subtle insults, procrastination, or intentional inefficiency, rather than addressing issues openly.

Patriarchy

Energy vampires tend to hold patriarchal views. Prioritizing male authority and dominance in social, political, and economic structures. This is not exclusive to men; women can uphold these views as well. Holding onto outdated views, affords them perceived protection regarding society as a whole. No matter how they choose to uphold these views, women will be consider second class citizen in comparison.

The Pick-Me Spirit

These energy vampires must be the center of attention at all cost. Often they will be the loudest in the room, and if not by voice, they will downplay what you are saying or talk over you, they will humiliate you and can be dangerous when they feel threatened. They tend to be very competitive and often needing their egos to be petted. They need a lot of validation and need to have a group that surrounds them. They quickly feel envious and jealous even if there is no immediate threat to them. Consequently, they also suffer at the hands of a lot of abuse, because their need for attention and to be picked, supersedes their safety and anyone else that is around them.

Pretty Envy

Energy vampires will have a predisposition to feel threatened by those who are naturally attractive. Often, they assume quite a lot of false truths, project their insecurities, and feel rejected by the attractive person, without giving the attractive person a chance to share who they are. Often attractive people are targeted by energy vampires. It is important to be kind to yourself; you are not as ugly as they treat you nor are you deserving of poor treatment.

Physical Abuse

Energy vampires deliberately hurt another person by using force. It can happen in various situations, within families, relationships, school, or work. Energy vampires do not care for the autonomy and sovereignty of others. While physical abuse is profoundly serious, it does not always come by way of hitting. Frequently, energy vampires will hurt or leave marks on the body that others cannot see. Such as using belts on the bottom, holding a person down until they give up or lose breath, or pinching, to hide their actions.

Pride

It is ok to be proud of who you are and your accomplishments. Energy vampires can be excessive in this nature. Displaying moral authority or portraying themselves as the authority over any given subject.

Projections

Energy vampires will project false narratives onto those around them. This reflects exactly what they themselves are guilty of. False narratives can produce internal nightmares if you believe what they are saying to be true. This is what causes the smoke between the mirrors. While what they project is not valid unless you accept it as truths, it does give you a glimpse of their internal world. The greatest sin you can commit to yourself is accepting others' projections as your truths. It is how you break your own heart, for this denies you, your light and your connection to Source.

Punishment

Energy vampires have a shared belief that others deserve to be punished for said crime and frequently prefer to be the punisher or significantly involved with judgment and the punishment.

Reactive Abuse

Energy vampires create a lot of chaos and offer few solutions to the nightmares and storms they create. The chaos can be insurmountable, undaunting, and unrelenting. Energy vampires lack boundaries and regularly do precisely what you ask them *not* to do.

They will create a lot of chaos, *"flying monkeys"* and dramas but offer minimal solutions to the chaos they create. Amused by the panic they entice in others. There is no end to the number of ways they will use reactive abuse to get the attention they feel entitled to. There is no reason for their actions other than to get a reaction from you. They will claim innocence or blame you for your response.

When you do not react, it confuses them and eventually drives them to anger. Sometimes, it will also cause them to be more threatening. No reaction is a reaction. It is pure defiance. *— A Battle of the Wills.*

Sadistic

Energy vampires have a taste for cruelty and are sadistic in nature. They get their pleasure from causing pain, suffering, or humiliation to others. This inclination is not always sexual in nature.

Served

Energy vampires have a need to be served by others; service to self is their highest calling. There is a preference to being served by the very people who they devalue or feel threatened by. It feeds their ego tremendously. At the core it is exploitive and a need to feel more powerful than another. This often goes hand in hand with the *"Cinderella Effect."*

Scape Goat

No matter what the setting is, energy vampires will choose a scape goat. This person will be blamed for things that are out of their control, often the center of *"humiliation rituals,"* and/or they are the topic of aggravation or disappointment. Frequently the scapegoat is the truth teller, holds a lot of light, and will highlight the shadows in others. Simply because they are everything an energy vampire is not. Even in silence, the scape goat will get kicked. They are used as a diversion tactic, to keep focus off what the energy vampire is doing.

Seen & Not Heard

In general, the vulnerable are easier targets: children, the elderly, the feeble, and those with less support and/or isolation. Energy vampires tend to have an overall belief that children should be seen and not heard. The sounds of children's bliss, creations, dance, imagination, laughter, or play will irritate such energies.

Self-Righteous

Energy vampires regularly hold self-righteous tendencies. They believe their values and morals are superior to those of others, accompanied by a sense of moral superiority. They lack basic empathy and understanding, as they focus on their own perceived righteousness rather than considering different perspectives and experiences.

Sexual Abuse

Sexual abuse and sexual exploitation are some of the most notable characteristics of more dangerous types of energy vampires. Sexual abuse can accrue in numerous ways, such as emotional manipulation, coercion, grooming or threats to justify abusive behavior. This will lead to significant emotional and psychological distress and the potential for soul loss.

Sexual abuse does not always include force. To get another to agree without force requires grooming, coercion, and manipulation. Sexual abuse can occur within various relationships, including those between family members, acquaintances, intimate partners, married couples, or strangers. Any time sexual activity occurs without consent; it is a form of sexual abuse. Even consent under manipulations, or pressure, is still sexual abuse.

For example, a partner using your body in the middle of the night when you are not awake and unable to consent. Another form is to deny touch in a private setting, but in public hyper touch and hyper sexualization The hyper sexualization in public is used to call in other vampires to take part in voyeurism.

Shallow

Often energy vampires are incredibly shallow and have an over inflated ego. There is not much thought or regard for anything that is not of their world. Conversations may be dull and surface level. Self-awareness may be limited to surface dislikes and preferences, but depth goes a miss. They tend walk hand in hand with the Adam & Eve spirits, the "me-me's" and the "pick-me" spirits. If you have any depth to you, you will suffocate in the shallow waters, best not swim where your heart does not sing.

Silent Treatment

Energy vampires will often use this tactic to devalue and to keep you in a state of confusion. It is their way of maintaining control through manipulation. Similarly, introverts and empaths are prone to needing a lot of rest from the outside world; you tell them apart by the intention and feelings behind the action or lack of action, especially when it is brought to their attention.

Sick Sense

Energy vampires lack empathy and self-awareness are poorly developed. Unlike Empaths who have a "sixth sense," energy vampires have a *"sick"* sense. Their actions of apathy, indifference, a taste for cruelty and humiliation of another gives them away. Ironically, some will even claim that they are emotionally intelligent, but at their core, they lack empathy.

Spiritual Abuse & Spiritual Narcissism

Spiritual abuse happens in numerous ways, such as emotional manipulation, coercion, grooming, sexual abuse, and threats. They use religious and spiritual teachings to justify abusive, grooming, or predatory behavior. It will lead to significant emotional and psychological distress in those who experience it.

"Just as narcissists believe that they are better than everyone else, spiritual narcissists believe that their spiritual wisdom and development is superior to others.' Spiritual narcissists boast about their spiritual or religious endeavors, including practices such as yoga, prayer, meditation, or knowledge of spiritual texts. Their presumption of superiority leads them to treat others with condescension. They manipulate others through twisting faith-based tenets, belief systems, or wield "forgiveness" as a weapon with those who question their beliefs." Suzanne Degges-White, PhD, LCPC, LPC, LMHC, NCC

Spiritual leaders of any practice have the potential to abuse those around them and their followers. Trust is given automatically and without question. These energy vampires hold authority, dominion, and significant influence. Using their knowledge, pietist nature, righteousness, and the need to be seen as *"good"* or *"nice"* as a mask, shield their behavior. More often than not, when a group perceives them as a *"good"* person they can be trickier to spot. The larger the group, the more they feed. The longer they feed, the longer they can mask.

Spite

Energy vampires can be incredibly petty and spiteful, especially if they feel wronged. Simply by not going along with their actions and ideals will make them feel attacked and offended. They play both offensive and defensive roles.

Splitting

Energy vampires will view people or situations in extremes. Everything is *"all good"* or *"all bad"* then manipulate others into taking sides.

Supremacy

Energy vampires have a belief system that they are superior or believe in having ultimate authority or control over others. Often based on factors such as disability, economic status, race, gender, orientation, or social status. Beliefs and actions that promote one group's dominance or superiority over others, which will lead to discrimination and inequality.

Stonewalling

Energy vampires will use stonewalling tactics as a deliberate act of resistance or avoidance. They will block communication or progress by refusing to engage, respond, or cooperate. They use silence in an evasiveness, or the outright dismissal of dialogue, creating an impassable barrier that halts resolution. This tactic is used strategically to gain control, deflect accountability, or frustrate the opposing party, but it often leads to heightened tension, and prolonged conflict. Those who are authoritarian in nature tend to employ this tactic. Simultaneously, they can become quite defensive when this behavior is mirrored back to them.

Survivors Envy

Some energy vampires take a particular dislike for those who survive an extreme situation, especially if you show up authentic and full of gratitude. Many times, extreme situations call forth a profound sense of gratitude and an abundance of joy for being alive. Energy vampires may or may not know your story, but they often disbelieve in your joyous or grateful nature. They can often be distrusting and even feel you are trying to manipulate a situation, simply by showing up as you are. Frequently feeling you are not suffering how they believe you should be suffering. They will attempt to dim your light by all means necessary, even causing situations that will create further suffering.

Threatening

Energy vampires often use threatening tactics when they feel entitled to get what they want. Threats are typically meant to intimidate, control, or manipulate someone into doing something, or to induce fear or anxiety about potential harm. This can be by way of direct or indirect threats or suggestions, against your vessel, towards your family or belongings.

Tokens

Energy vampires like their shiny new things and have an eye for the exotic. For something to be considered exotic, there is rareness. Usually because they were endangered or because of extinction due to displacement or poaching behavior.

They will see the value in you, though they will not value you. They will mishandle your spirit on the one hand, but in public they will tokenize you. This will call in other energy vampires to feed off your energy. This can be especially dangerous and problematic for the LGBTQ+ and those who have an ethnic and/or Indigenous background to be considered exotic.

Trauma Bonding

Trauma bonding happens organically and can be very unhealthy if a pair is united solely on a bond based on past traumas. Creating an emotional connection through cycles of abuse and reconciliation, fostering dependency and making it difficult for you to leave.

Triangulation

When energy vampires feel they need vindication, they will bring a third party into conflicts or dynamics to create tension, competition, or dependency.

Wealth Hoarding

The idea of money is another great illusion that energy vampires use to control the masses. The very obscenely rich, meaning the 0.01% who actively engage in genocide, monopoly of over resources, and war. Money is meaningless to them. What is of value is your energy. They harvest it through fear, propaganda, and distractions. All of which keeps you disconnected from Source and in a state of panic and suffering. They are the most apathetic; consumption and service to self is all they know.

Weaponized Incompetence

Energy vampires will weaponize incompetence, which refers to the tactic where someone pretends to be incapable or unskilled to avoid responsibility or tasks.

Weaponized Labor

While labor is how businesses maintain their goods and services, Energy vampires will often weaponize your energy, focus and time. Purposefully understaffing, long hours, little regard for safety, and the worst participating in slave labor. The financial gain supersedes their employees and their customers. Wealth hoarding at its finest. They reek of apathy and colonization spirits. They require a well-assimilated and domesticated population to maintain control. It becomes quite challenging for you to support your spiritual body while also maintaining the required structures from those in charge.

Weaponized Tears

Energy vampires will weaponize their tears. This is a strategic use of emotional outbursts, particularly crying, to manipulate situations or gain sympathy, and/or to shift the blame and focus. Their tears dry up as soon as they meet their goals, and their mood will be as if nothing happened at all. Women are prone to employing this tactic, and white women's tears are the most dangerous to those of color, especially in public and even more dangerous for men of color. It is not solely a female weapon of choice; men also use this tactic as well.

Weaponized Speech

Energy vampires will weaponize language. This is precisely what "*spell work*" is. They use language and voice to hypnotize by dominating the airtime. It comes in the forms of talking over, rapid and repetitive speech. When an idea is repeated more than seven times, in a short period, this is the narrative they are trying to control and becomes intentional programming. They attempt to assert their Will over another by way of dominance. This is where they purposefully sow confusion, chaos, fear and eventually anger. They will also use their voice to project louder to call in authority, dominance, or to invoke a specific feeling by purposefully poking at your pain points.

Weaponized Victimization

While there is tremendous hardship when you are at the receiving end of trauma, and it requires a variety of healing modalities to move the energies through your body, some energy vampires will use this to manipulate a situation. They tend to revert to this portion of their life anytime they are being held accountable for their wrong doings.

White Fragility

Some energy vampires will show signs of white fragility and will defend the stance that there is no such thing as racism and inequality. Coined, by Dr. Robin DiAngelo, and it refers to the defensive reactions or discomfort that some white individuals may experience when confronted with issues related to race and racism. This defensiveness arises when their racial identity or privilege is challenged, making it difficult for them to engage in meaningful conversations about race.

White Supremacy & Zionism

Energy vampires tend to hold a belief system or ideology that promotes the idea that white or 'pure' people are superior to those of other racial backgrounds. This includes discriminatory and prejudiced beliefs and practices that maintain the dominance of white individuals and communities over others.

This ideology is associated with racial discrimination, inequality, and various forms of injustice. While not spoken outright, they tend to hold eugenic ideals at the core of their beliefs and is usually employed by way of policies or decisions that provoke genocide and war.

Whispers

While loud rapid speech can be assaulting. Energy vampires will also employ whispers. Speaking false truths, *"casting shadow,"* wishing ill, anger or any other projection in a low tone, just out of earshot. Sometimes, they are entirely unaware that their parasites have come to the surface, while other times it is very intentional.

Withholding

Energy vampires will deliberately refuse to share information, affection, resources, or support to manipulate or control others.

Wrath

Energy vampires will display wrath, especially when their perceived ideals are called into question, or they feel they have been wronged. In comparison, anger is an emotion that is needed to heal at times, wrath on the other hand, calls for revenge. Sometimes they are methodical, other times it is an instant and immediate reaction to a perceived slight.

Chapter 10: Spiritual Awakening

"I AM" ©*Zoila Luz Rosario Masiak 2024*

The spiritual awakening is a long journey of Self Awareness, Consciousness, Remembrance, the Return to Self, Self-Actualization, Rebirth, Resurrection, and Ascension. It is a personal journey of evolution, self-mastery, and spiritual growth. It involves elevating and expanding your awareness and consciousness to higher levels of observations, *inner-standing*, existence, and vibration, while also shedding your limiting beliefs and programming. An expansion of authenticity, compassion, empathy, unconditional love, the interconnection of all that is and the ability to commune with Source. An understanding of the multi-faceted fractal of life, the oneness and that there is never one outward expression, but an infinite expansion in every possible direction. The journey is not linear and most certainly not singular. At times it may feel like there is no relevance, because all that is, what was, and what will come are all simultaneous. Ascension goes hand in hand with the desire for liberation and sovereignty for all living *be-ings,* not just your own.

The Ascension process is not a singular event. It happens over a lifetime of intentional healing, deconstruction, studying, *inner-standing* and integration. It is a continuous pursuit, and full of repeated lessons that will circle back around until you learn the lesson well. Then you will be tested. If you are able to acknowledge them for what they are, they will not hold you back because you will have learned the lesson. You learn to sidestep the chaos of others and learn to be a more equipped driver of your vehicle. With every mask revealed to yourself, and for every mask that you shed, you will shift consciousness.

For Rebirth to happen, it requires intentional conscious effort and action. You will have many revelations and shifts in consciousness, some more rapid than others; and you will go through several seven-year cycles. It takes seven years for your body to replace every cell. It is a lifetime worth of work, encompassing every fiber of your *be-ing.*

The journey to return to the body can be as emotional and heavy as the trip out of the body. More often than not, it takes longer than the initial event to come back to self. The journey back to self is a painful one but fear not; discovery is a beautiful adventure that frees your spirit from that which binds you.

Tower moments will clear anything and everything out of the way to give room for growth. Tower moments are life altering, with repeated lessons thrown into the mix. If you do not repeat, you can skip ahead, so to speak. Tower moments will push you into the Dark Knight of the Soul, the darkest time in your life and the most isolating. Here the ego will shatter, an ego death if you will. You will most certainly mourn the version of you that no longer fits. As you expand, your ego will have to take a back seat, and this can be very confrontational if you are not ready to let go of the once-was.

Learn to see yourself as the sweet innocent child you came into this world as. Learn to give yourself Grace. Not all deeds are done by force. Time and time again, misdeeds are done in the dark. Do not waste your breath with things that do not mirror your sweeter self.

Remember, energy vampires can mimic the light but cannot maintain it. Do not blame yourself; these misdeeds have infected most of our society. Instead acknowledge, and accept situations for what they are, cleanse, purge, put one foot in front of the other and let go. Thank the Universe for the lesson, learn the lesson, and do your best not to repeat it. You will find that future events will test you, but with the tools you pick up along the way, you find that if you learned the lesson, you will minimize the harshness and move the energies out quickly.

For every mask you wear, you must deconstruct and take it off. You will experience a mourning for the old self but a greater appreciation and tenderness for who you are becoming. These moments will require you to conserve your essence. Grounding, good spiritual hygiene practices, cutting cords from what does not serve your highest good, purging, calling your Soul back, transmuting, and giving yourself time to integrate will help speed up the process. Keep your vessel clear of as many poisons as possible; so that you may make room for the Light. It takes seven years to replace every cell in your body. Stick to your healing for seven years and rebirth is inevitable.

Know Thyself

"There are only ever two lessons you learn from those around you. You either learn how to be or you learn how not to be." -Nana, Alejandra Encinas Dominguez. In your first encounter with another, you are introduced to their egos, masks, shadows and ancestors first. The one that protects and guards them from this world. *–Know thyself, and you come to know what you are, and what you are not. Who you will and will not tango with.*

The difference between "understanding" and *"inner-standing"* is that understanding is of thought, and mental capacities only. However, *inner-standing:* is felt in your heart and throughout. To *inner-stand*, you must really sit with how something affects your body. This is the difference between logic base linear thinking, and intuition, though *inner-standing* encompasses both thought and feeling. To know your intuition is to know your body. Learning your own body, intuitions, and triggers is the best way to unravel the chaos and nightmares created by apathy spirits and energy vampires. The experiences will be different from one individual to another. However, what is not different is that your empathy and your senses are indeed spiritual gifts that allow you to alchemize, observe, discern, heal and to keep yourself and others safe.

Knowing your triggers and managing your vessel is essential to determine if you are experiencing serious health or mental complications, ascension symptoms, or spiritual attacks. It is vital to know yourself. For if you do not know yourself inside and out, the world most assuredly will tell you who they think you are and what you are worth. – *You are not who they say you are. You are who you think and say you are. For what you think, you speak. For what you speak, you become.*

Scanning

Scanning your vessel will help manage some, if not most, of the internal discomforts of this world. The less emotional, mental, and spiritual pain you are in, the more you will gain incredible amounts of energy, strength, and time because your muscles will be less rigid in nature. For example, compare buffalo to wagyu to American cattle.

Pain and discomfort in your body is your intuition. It will tell you where you need to pay attention. When you find the source of pain, you can help move through your body. When you scan, you want to make sure you scan all four bodies (emotional, mental, physical, and spiritual). Sometimes, the pain is physical and needs attention immediately. The mental, emotional, and spiritual bodies can be complicated to identify. Shadow Work is excellent for such internal discoveries.

Symptoms of A Spiritual Awakening:

The symptoms associated with the spiritual or energy changes that I have found to be true. These symptoms can vary widely from person to person, but they are generally seen as indicators of a shift in consciousness, energy, and vibration. It is important to note that these symptoms are not necessarily negative, although they can be challenging. Make sure you have ruled out all other health concerns, as some of these symptoms can also be related to more serious health issues.

Body Temperature, Blood Pressure, and Heart Rate

Fluctuations in blood pressure and temperature, including feeling unusually cold or hot for no apparent reason. Intermittent or increased heart palpitations, even in the absence of cardiac issues. During times of stress, blood pressure and heart rate can decrease or increase.

When you meditate and practice shallow breathing, you can momentarily lower your heart rate and blood pressure. In these silent still moments, the in-between becomes very noticeable. Time slows down and the ability to track fast-moving objects becomes apparent, such as a fly or gnat.

Much of your inner knowing comes in these moments of stillness. Creating connection with your higher self as well as non-human energies, channeling, downloads, and visions become easier to *inner-stand*.

Challenges with Grounding

Struggle with grounding or feeling disoriented when navigating between different states of consciousness. It is of the utmost importance that you learn to stay grounded in both worlds.

It is easy to get lost in the sauce and lose all sense of time. These moments can be incredibly challenging if you are not fully grounded with your vessel and our Earth Mother.

Detoxification & Purging

As you undergo energetic and emotional clearing, you may experience detoxification symptoms, such as uncontrollable tears or even uncontrollable laughter, fatigue, headaches, and gastric disturbances. Keeping the vessel free of dramas and stresses that are not your own, makes the energies easier to transmute and move out of the body quickly.

Accepting situations as they are, rather than how you wish for them to be. Learn to let go and detach from what was, any expectations, what is not yours, or what does not serve your highest potential.

Allow yourself time to process and feel everything fully. Often you will have repeated emotions about a situation, but as you intentionally let go, they begin to dissolve and so do the stored memories in the body. Be patient if things come back around, that is your spirit and body telling you where you need to focus your light and healing.

Digestive Disturbances

Changes in digestion, including bloating, gas, diarrhea, or constipation. Food and multiple chemical sensitivities and dietary changes. Tasting the misery that the food was produced with or made with becomes palpable.

Even the smells of foods you once loved can cause your stomach to turn. Preparing your food in ceremony, as well as keeping your diet clean, will combat many of these sensations.

Emotional Turbulence

Emotional ups and downs will occur as old emotional wounds surface for healing. This can result in mood swings ranging from anger, anxiety, depression, imposter syndrome, and moments of deep introspection. Every range of emotions can occur, and the shifts can be very rapid.

Give yourself Grace, and don't fight it. Surrender, but do not get lost. Breathe and let go. I know that this can feel minimizing, but it will not serve you to have your world stuck in the past. Eventually you will recycle enough until these emotions no longer live inside your body, nor will you remember.

Spiritual psychosis is a very real experience; therefore, grounding is of the utmost importance. Avoid taking in too much spiritual content at once, without fully processing and integrating. Be mindful of who you are learning from because their shadows can greatly sway your internal dialogue if you are not conscious of all your thoughts and actions. Truly make an effort to know thyself. What is of you, and what is not? It will make it easier to navigate through the storms of your spiritual awakening. Energetically, it can be genuinely gruesome and exhausting to break through the fog.

Learning to navigate the storms will help you sail through and step aside when you notice a repeated lesson. Lessons become less painful over time, as you learn to navigate the stormy waters.

Expanded State of Awareness & Consciousness

You will find that you become highly aware of your inner world and the observers of others. You will find most things in our modern society to be dull and uninteresting. Such as drinking or nightlife. This is because your energy is not going towards your path and purpose. None of it is as fulfilling as your spirit's divine purpose.

As you shed old habits and ideals internally, they will manifest outwardly into your physical world. Those who were once close will vibrate away. Do not let it hurt too much. Realize, you've learned the lesson, and you are being protected. Your energy is your own and you get to do more of what you love, rather than what you dread. You will find some of your greatest blessings will be in these moments. *–Divine Protection is a blessing in disguise. Embrace it.*

When you become aware of more, you also must process and integrate more. You will discover and cultivate your spiritual gifts in these moments. You will find there are days when you just need rest. Honor that in yourself.

Headaches

Intense and/or frequent headaches, are sometimes described as pressure or tension headaches. These can be accompanied by dizziness or lightheadedness.

This world is so chaotic, and our body becomes very keen to those energies that disrupt the peace within. Sensory overload affects us all. The ability to identify and distinguish between the triggers quickens the healing time.

Heightened Sensitivity

Sensations of internal vibrations or electrical currents moving through the body, such as a buzzing or tingling sensation. Increased sensitivity to energies, emotions, stimuli, and environmental factors: such as allergies, chemicals, electronics, or electromagnetic fields (EMFs).

Heightened sensory perception: to light, smells, sounds, tastes, and touch. Colors appear more vivid, and sounds may be more acute and more distinguishable. Changes in vision, such as seeing flickering lights, colors, or patterns when meditating or closing the eyes.

Broader scope in peripheral vision as well as the ability to track the movements of smaller *be-ings* like fruit flies. Time can feel like it slows down when you are tracking fast moving entities.

Heightened empathy, intuition, and psychic abilities. Increased perceptions of the energies of any *be-ing*, not just your own.

Grief & Rage

Make no mistake, the spiritual awakening is a messy one. Do not let them fool you into thinking something is wrong with you because you are not always full of love and light. You are processing deep pain. You will experience a great deal of rage as things bubble up to the surface.

You will come to know that Rage is Grief. Grief for the injustice of your experiences and your fiercest protector of your inner child and light. You will also discover that rage has a divine purpose. When focused it can propel you in the direction you wish to be. Though, you must not let it engulf you or control you. You will experience grief and all its infinite wisdoms.

Grief for the things that happened to you.

Grief for all the missed opportunities.

Grief for what you tolerated.

Grief for what you did not stop.

Grief for what you cannot control.

Grief for the inner teenager.

Grief for the inner child.

Grief for the things you did.

Grief for what you did not do.

Grief for family and friends.

Grief for those you've lost.

Grief for your ancestors.

Grief for the old self that you are shedding.

Internal & External Conflicts

The process of shedding old beliefs and behaviors can create inner conflicts as you confront your ego, attachments, limiting beliefs, conditioning, and programming.

Your relationships will undergo transformation. Some connections may deepen, while others may dissolve. Detaching, when necessary, will ease the energy drain and propel you where you need to be.

Lucid Dreams

Lucid dreams are not your ordinary dreams. Lucid dreams feel no different than when you are awake. You will feel and experience these dreams just like your mundane physical life. Meaning you can talk, taste, hear, smell, touch, and perceive. In these spaces, you can control your dreams.

As your dreams become more regular and vivid; they carry with them deep symbolic and spiritual messages. Downloads, Visions, and prophecies become more frequent. Learning to control your dreams while you are in a dream world is an ability you can acquire. Your dreams cannot hurt you, though they can be scary if you are not prepared and if your mind is not calm.

Magnetism

The light from your energetic field has the ability to shift rooms, even before you enter a space. You will find that your light burns those who are not living in their authentic truth and will shy away from eye contact. It is both magnetic and a repellent. You will even find that electronics will act unusual in your presence. Learning to hold your energetic boundaries is especially important, for yourself and for others. It is incredibly easy to attract and create unnecessary chaos if you are not fully aware.

You will find that your light will act like a magnet. It has the potential to call in all manner of *be-ings* and chaos alike. Everything from animals, to bugs, to children and energy vampires are no different. It is a balance to both take up space and to respect space. In time, you will learn how to master your gifts.

Physical Symptoms

Unexplained aches and pains, digestive disturbances, and fatigue often occur, right before there is a shift in consciousness. As the chains break, all four bodies become lighter and stronger.

Once fully processed, the pains of the past slowly melt away. Even after the pain is released, you must care for your vessel so that the pain does not settle in your bones. You will have to actively cleanse, maintain, purge, and transmute. Your body is slower than your consciousness. It can become rigid when triggered. It will take time to master your vessel.

Gaining physical strength, speed, agility, quicker processing time, and the ability to keep the higher self in the body. This happens because you no longer carry the tension in your body. Just like for strength training, when you wear weights on your ankles, and once you take them off, you gain speed. It is the same thing, but with your energy and essence. You will find that you are capable of so much more and do so with ease.

As you become spiritually stronger, so does your health. Clear skin, increased muscle tone, and spontaneous healing will occur. Others may not recognize you, and even you may not recognize the outdated version of yourself.

Sleep Disturbances

Changes in sleep patterns, including difficulty falling asleep, waking up frequently during the night, or needing longer than normal night's rest and naps.

Spiritual Insights

Increased spiritual insights, realizations, and epiphanies will occur during the ascension process. These insights will lead to a deeper understanding of your purpose, and connection to Source. You become the master and observer of not only your higher self but also the ability to observe others without interference to their sovereignty.

Third Eye

Sensation in the area of the third eye. Tickling sensation on the roof of the mouth straight to the third eye and through the crown and above, with an extended sensation in your forehead. As consciousness expands, the tickle will move to a pressure that will move to the top of the crown and expand outwards.

You will find when you focus. You will feel this expansion until you feel it throughout your forehead. Experiencing higher states of consciousness, such as states of bliss, unity, and oneness, in meditation or when experiencing downloads, telepathy, or visions.

Time Warp

Changes in the perception of time, such as: time seeming to speed up or slow down, Deja-vu and perception in shift of vibration and the shift in consciousness of others. This is where you experience an entire shift in state of consciousness and so have the neighboring realities. As the veil thins, time will feel like it speeds up. This is because as truths are revealed, it also creates chaos. Things are no longer what they once were, or at least how you perceived them to be, and your consciousness must shift to keep up.

Time disruptions can be seen in the difference of times between the country and cities. As the coming and goings can be experienced slower or faster depending on location. This is because there are more chaotic energies in the city and there is more to observe, experience, and digest in all four of your bodies.

Gravitational Time Dilation is the phenomenon where time moves slower in stronger gravitational fields and faster in weaker ones. Rooted in Einstein's General Theory of Relativity, it reveals that time is not fixed but bends under the weight of gravity itself. Near massive celestial bodies, like black holes or even deep valleys on Earth, the fabric of time stretches, causing moments to elongate — while at higher altitudes, such as mountaintops or cities, time ticks by at a slightly faster pace. More than a scientific principle, it is a reminder that reality itself is fluid.–*Even time bows to the weight of existence.*

Quantum Immortality

Those who have had NDEs may experience Quantum Immortality. Quantum immortality is the idea that consciousness never truly dies — it simply shifts. This theory suggests that at every moment of potential death, reality splits, and the observer always continues in the timeline where they survive. To those left behind, it may seem like an ending, but for the one experiencing it, existence never breaks — it only moves. The body may fade in one reality, but the essence carries on, waking up in the version of the universe where they remain. Whether viewed through the lens of quantum mechanics or spiritual truth, the core remains the same. – *Your spirit is pure infinite energy and never really dies.*

In my experience, this is where I felt I had a choice, and it has happened on several occasions. When your soul leaves your body and you become bathed in the light, some may have a choice or feel pulled back to their bodies. When your spirit returns, almost everything is different. There is a period of adjustment. Every time we have a shift in awareness and elevation in consciousness time speeds up, and then our physical body must catch up and rest.

Chapter 11: Ascension

"Returned" ©*Zoila Luz Rosario Masiak 2024*

The North Bound Expedition

I have journeyed quite a lot during my time here on Earth. I've come to know that part of my purpose was to experience the Great Divide. Gifting me wisdoms so that I may aid others in seeing through the illusions of the veil from the perspective of near-death experiences. To be the walking embodiment of Grace and Miracles; Proof that the Creator, Christ Consciousness, and Divine Magic exist. The Journey to Remembrance has been quite turbulent — *Indeed, it has been a heavy cross to bear.*

Like Peter Pan — unnaturally sweet, fiercely protecting my innocence to the best of my ability, holding onto my Light for dear life — I traversed the rainbow bridge, encouraging those who I can, to join me in the greatest adventure ever there was. The greatest journey anyone will ever take is from the head to the heart, bridging the divide and to walk in harmony. — *The Northbound Expedition of Becoming.*

The night my dreams returned, I received visions from The Dire Wolf and The White Rabbit; *I had to face myself.* Then came a vision of seven past lives, urging me to Remember: *Remembrance.* Only then did I receive visions from Spider Woman that revealed to me the truth about *The Evils of Apathy;* I had to return to the Land, return to innocence, and to do that, I had to heal up.

I understood that in ten years, collective communities would be needed, and I had to prepare. In 2018, my boys and I left the industrialized Tidewater region and settled in the southern Appalachian Region of Virginia. While I knew a *Great Mass Awakening* was coming, I never believed I would survive to witness such a miracle.

Over the past seven years, I have been healing from all that has been taken from me. A series of unfortunate events and energy vampires had drained me of my essence and light. Having my breath stolen in countless ways and revealing how the spirit travels.

My guides revealed to me that I had been held captive by grief and rage, too weak to speak. It was they who made me realize I was never as ugly or as bad as I had been treated. That I had to face myself and treat myself as I would as a child. Slowly but surely, as I followed my spirit guides and visions, I started to heal. After years of continuous work, I experienced spontaneous healing. My angelic wings emerged. I saw all my journeys in and out of my body. It was then, and only then, that I realized the veil is truly palpable, and I knew the way through. I understood then, as I do now, that I must share these truths.

The last four years of my seven-year Reawakening Journey has felt like a Rebirth, Resurrection, and Ascension. I have changed so much that not even my family and friends scarcely recognized me when I returned. Confirming my metamorphosis. These are some of the truths I have uncovered through this quest and the many side quests along the way. Because of the nature of side quests, the phases may seem out of order to your perspective. Only agree to what resonates and feels harmonic in your own vessel.

While I cannot physically hold everyone's hands through the transition, I set the intention to share my heartfelt consciousness, so that some of my words will ring true, to act as a beacon of Light, freeing those who I can.

Breaking Chains & Angelic Wings

Self-mastery is a never ending quest of mastering awareness of these aspects leading you to true sovereignty, healing and embodiment. We are all multi-dimensional and hold multiple ways of *be-ing*. No one person is front facing only. Like an egg, our vessel is a shell that protects the Light until the day comes when we are ready to break free from the shell and emerge bringing forth our higher self to the surface. Your spirit is the eternal spark of the Divine within you, a limitless essence that connects you to the Creator and Source.

Surrounding it all is your energetic field, made up of countless energetic threads, woven with the stories of you. The lessons of your journey, essence, *emotions*, *dis-eases*, ancestors, past lives, spirit guides, spiritual gifts, your Light and shadows, parasites, karma the seeds of your manifestations, antenna, compass, vibrations and frequency. This field holds the truth of your past, present, and your potential future — *A reminder that you are both the creator and the creation, infinite potential.*

As you commit to your healing and authentic self, you are reestablishing and strengthening your connection to your higher self and Source. You are also elevating your consciousness and vibration. The healing journey and the return to self is not linear and most certainly is not a singular event.

You will be presented with similar lessons and tests until you learn how to move accordingly. The tests are often not as hard as the initial lessons, but they can feel overwhelming as they frequently call forth past burdens. Every lesson is an opportunity to engage with your *Free Will, The Muscle of Choice.*

Every time you experience a break in one of the links of the chain, you must handle yourself as you would an infant. Eat clean, rest, engage in spiritual bathing, ground yourself, and give yourself a lot of Grace. Honor and respect your boundaries. Protect your energy. Do not engage with anything that drains you. Give people space and give yourself space as well. Avoid getting winded by arguments or excessive chatter. Do not let people stand too close or become too comfortable taking your breath away. Simply stepping back from a situation will create space. You must be deeply rooted while you are healing. Avoid those who hurt you during these moments. You will be tender, and it will be easy for others to touch those pain points when you are raw.

With each phase, there will be a burst of energy in all four bodies — a mishmash of feelings hitting at once: grief, rage, panic, anxiety, excitement, extraordinary experiences, epiphanies, enlightenment, tears, laughter, changes in the realities around you, as well as spontaneous healing.

Pay close attention to your body and its triggers; they will help strengthen your discernment. Understanding your vessel and spirit aids in your ability to understand what lies outside of you. Deconstruction is vital to understanding your energies, breaking spells, and experiencing Rebirth.

Anything that engages in the senses has the power to invoke energy and memory. You can easily become consumed or lost in the ethers; where your body remains in one place while your consciousness drifts elsewhere. In this state, your ego and shadows tend to drive your vessel.

You're more vulnerable to accidents, illnesses, trickster spirits, parasites, and spiritual attacks. The sooner you recognize and deconstruct these triggers and patterns, the better equipped you will be the next time a trigger arises. This is an opportunity to sidestep a difficult lesson.

Spirit knows not of time nor space. It is a lifelong pursuit of self-mastery. Remember, it is your vessel, your spirit, and your responsibility to take care of them both. Give yourself Grace, time to deconstruct, process, and integrate. Avoid biting off more than you can digest. Stay on top of healthy eating, hydration, rest, grounding, and create good spiritual hygiene practices that work best for you.

Try not to take in too much spiritual content at once. There is a plethora of spiritual practices, healing modalities, and opinions out there. It is easy to get "lost in the sauce" if you are not grounded and deeply rooted in who you are.

The Difference Between

Self-awareness is the fundamental building blocks to your emotional intelligence and consciousness. Being self-aware does not necessarily mean you are responding with intentional thought or action.

Consciousness is the evolving awareness of existence, the lens through which you perceive, think, and create reality. It is the level of active perception and participation you operate from. Consciousness is layered, ranging from basic self-awareness to divine awareness. It determines how you engage with reality and evolve through experiences.

Vibration is your state of consciousness that you momentarily agree to. You will stay in that state until your ability to shift perspectives and consciousness.

Frequency is your momentary reflection of your emotional, mental, and spiritual alignment; when you reside in the energy of authenticity, empathy, bliss and unconditional love, you will come to know miracles. Likewise, if you reside in anger or fear, your body will feel pain and whatever state you are in, you will project your internal world outwardly.

The ego is the construct of identity, the aspect of the mind that defines "I" in relation to the external world. It is not inherently bad but serves as a necessary interface between the soul and the physical experience. Like an egg, the ego is the outer shell of your vessel. How people perceive you and how you express. It is meant to guard and protect the innocent self, the sweeter self, the joy, the *Light*. The ego enjoys all that is physical and dramas, as that is what it excites it most. However, when left unchecked, ego can disconnect and make you forget your higher self and become a barrier to your growth, clinging to separateness, superiority, or fear-based survival patterns. You will always meet anothers' ego first before you come to know their spirit.

The Alter Ego is a created or projected version of oneself, often used to navigate different roles in life. It can be empowering (a mask for confidence, strength, or protection) or deceptive (a distortion of self to manipulate or to escape truths). Alter Egos can be tools of transformation or illusions that distance us from authenticity.

The Subconscious is the vast, hidden realm of the mind where memories, programming, and deep-seated beliefs reside. It shapes habits, emotions, and instincts without conscious thought. Most traumas, fears, and limiting beliefs are rooted here, often influencing choices without one's active awareness. Healing the subconscious is key to growth and sovereignty.

The Shadow is the combination of the ego, alter ego, subconscious, and any emotions that have the potential to possess the mind with fear, doubt, rage, lust, or any other emotions that disconnects your higher self and the outer world, until you are ready to emerge. The ego is the outer shell, the subconscious is the inner shell, and the shadow surrounds the yolk. All are tasked to protect the yolk, your Light.

The Soul is your eternal essence, the unique divine spark that carries wisdom across lifetimes. It is the experience of existence, learning through cycles of birth, death, and rebirth. The soul desires expansion, truth, and evolution, but it can be weighed down by ego, and subconscious wounds.

The Higher Self is the fully awakened aspect of the soul, existing beyond gender, duality and illusion. It is the bridge between human limitations and divine wisdom. Always guiding from a place of unconditional love, it provides insight, nudges us toward growth, and helps align our soul with its highest potential and purpose.

The Creator is the divine architect of all existence — the force that initiates life, consciousness, and universal laws. Unlike Source, which is pure, boundless essence, the Creator actively shapes reality but does not maintain or control it, as it can only create. Demanding authority or obedience would strip you of your birthright: the vessel, Free Will, your Light, and your empathy to guide you; are all gifts from the Creator, to experience life. We are the mirrors to one another and the Creator alike.

We are the eyes of the observer, observing itself. A witness to its existence and to our own. To know thyself, is to know the Creator. To know the Creator is to be known by the Creator.

Source is the infinite source of energy of all existence — the absolute, formless essence from which all things arise and to which all things return. It is the purest state of divine energy, beyond name, form, and structure. While the Creator is the architect, Source is the endless ocean of *be-ing.*

Piercing the Veil

In my journey so far, I have found each state offers a unique perspective and experiences, guiding me through different phases of self-awareness and spiritual growth. Everyone will experience this slightly different. As you move through this process, you will gradually lighten your load, shedding old patterns and limiting beliefs, while raising your overall vibration. This transformation is not just about a shift in mindset but a complete realignment of your *be-ing,* affecting your thoughts, emotions, energy, focus, and physical well-being. These phases are not absolutes, merely keys to aid you in your journey.

As you begin to awaken, you will realize that this is a multi-tiered process, moving from the subconscious to consciousness and ultimately Ascension. It is a continual unfolding, where every step forward unlocks deeper layers of understanding, helping you reconnect with your higher self and Source. Each stage serves as a steppingstone, leading you closer to your authentic essence and purpose. Self-mastery is a never-ending quest, of mastering awareness of these aspects leading you to healing, true sovereignty, and embodiment.

The journey is not a singular event and most certainly not a linear one. You will find your conscious skipping around until you are able to control your inner world. This quest will require you to do more than look at the waves. You must actively learn to open each world and dive deep and deconstruct so that you may find your way back again.

You will discover all aspects of yourself. For each world you enter, you must fully deconstruct to be fully aware of the vastness that is you. Entering these worlds, you can no longer stay in shallow waters. These waters are quite deep, and you can become lost in their depths. This is where you must be like a whale. Surfacing for oxygen, when need be, you must make continuous efforts to be fully present, even while asleep. Dream world is multi-dimensional as well and can be quite treacherous if you cannot find your way back peacefully.

As you dive deep, when you surface, your consciousness becomes elevated with each deep dive you take. There is no end to this evolution once you start. You learn that you are able *to walk on water,* observing the observer and that of another, and you will be able to move through masses with ease. Here you will find that Christ Consciousness resides in these waters. This is an expansion of you, bringing forth your Higher Self to the surface as it can no longer reside unbeknownst to you. In doing so, when you do walk among the masses, they will part like the Red Sea, respecting your Light. Some may not be aware of your presence at all, but your energy will supersede you and many will unconsciously move even with their heads down.

Here is where you find others in their own hell. Many who reside in apathy do not speak the language of empathy. They will not even be able to hear you, as their smoke and veil covering their eyes is quite dense.

Do not take it personally and do not burn yourself by staying where you do not belong.

The 1st Phase: The Catalyst

Tower moments are moments of utter collapse, where everything around you is uprooted, becoming a catalyst for transformation. However, the catalyst is so great, it is an earth-shattering event. One so massive, you hit point zero and awaken to many of the illusions within the matrix of society and yourself. Everything you thought you knew turns out to be different from what it was. Like a star, you reach critical mass, a supernova — your world collapses into a black hole. The inward collapse becomes a hellish void of nothingness. While it may feel never-ending, it does end once you face yourself.

This is the moment where you say, *enough is enough,* and you choose healing. You choose your spirit despite everything. This shift can be brought on by multiple moments or one single event. Either way, there is no turning back. The journey to self and self-actualization becomes the focus. Intentional healing and a quest for understanding and a much needed *inner-standing* take the lead as you realize you must face yourself— the good, the bad, the indifferent, the ancestors, the tricksters, the parasites, the masks, and the shadows.

Although this event is incredibly painful, and may take years to overcome, you begin to shift your focus. Taking control of your subconscious mind, you see that every event after this becomes a steppingstone towards growth. You start to notice cycles in the lessons: first comes the lesson, then understanding, then the test, then testimonies, then knowledge, then wisdoms, more tests though they become less harsh, then embodiment, eventually master of your vast inner world, then teacher.

How you respond determines how long the pain will last. Over time, you learn the patterns and develop discernment. Sometimes, simply recognizing and understanding the energy is enough to release it from your body. When similar situations arise, you become less likely to engage because you've already learned the lesson. Tests will still come, but if you've mastered the lesson, the outcome is usually not as bad as you imagined.

You realize that you must master your own mind and heart. You may find yourself on countless side quests, searching for answers. This was the point where I found my way to elders, who insisted that I ground myself before learning anything else.

The 2nd Phase: Leaning Into Your Intuition

Our modern world often encourages us to ignore our intuition. We are not taught its necessity nor its practical applications. If anything, we are told to dismiss it entirely. This is where the disconnection and masking begin. However, at this point, you must lean in rather than turn away. Like a newborn learning to walk, your muscles may feel weak, and your sight obscured by the veil and the smoke and mirrors of the outside world's illusions. Yet, as you heal and call your soul back to you, this muscle will strengthen.

The 3rd Phase: Layered Consciousness

Like a basement, you are filled to the brim with experiences both neatly stacked and tossed about and some boxes overflowing.

When you open the basement door, you must be brave and face those dark stairs and you must do more than acknowledge look and say, *"It's a mess!"* You must have the fortitude to walk those unlit stairs and open each box tenderly. Reorganizing and discarding what no longer serves you. It can be a very undaunting task, though you know your spirit desperately needs it, to make room for the light.

You realize there are multi-dimensional aspects of yourself; all residing in their own energies and consciousness, each having feminine energies (creation, empathy, intuition, and harmony) and masculine energies (focus, linear thinking, forward driven), negative energies (fear anger, chaos, nightmares) and positive energies (hope, joy, wisdom, solutions and sweet dreams), with the ability to move through space and time bringing forth memories of old and future scenarios.

The 4th Phase: Layered Awareness

Imagine your body is a van. This is your ***Physical Awareness,*** it has all manner of needs that are purely mechanical, and it requires you to maintain it. It has a dashboard that makes you aware of its needs.

This includes your ***Functional Awareness***. These are your gauges and are autonomic in nature — taste, smell, touch, hearing, proprioception (external sensors), vestibular (internal balance), gut, heart, temperature, pressure, motion, light, chemical/hormonal, and spatial awareness.

You also have a built-in compass, multi-functional GPS unit, radio and antenna which requires **Empathy and Intuition** to tune into your **Frequency Awareness**. The antenna is your direct connection to Our Earth Mother and Source alike. Your GPS unit and radio allow you to tune into the energies of your body, and your external world. They work best when harmonious, but you have yet to learn how to tune into and use the dashboard, gauges, navigation system, or radio.

Now, imagine your van is packed to the brim with layered attributes. Some are more aware than others. Each has its own way of being, and depending on who is driving your van, that reality will be presented to the rest of the world.

You have a driver, **Unconscious Awareness,** who physically moves and operates this van. The driver isn't paying attention to all the gauges, so they are missing a lot of information — *sleep driving*, if you will. This is quite important because you are moving from a state of reactive unconsciousness to self-aware to consciousness to self-actualization, and it requires a lot of willpower to move out of a state of unconsciousness.

Now imagine that you have several passengers with you. The first is your shotgun rider, **Navigational Awareness**, who aids by reading a paper map, but they take a lot of detours since the map is not as detailed as your GPS and radio. They're supposed to help you see the traffic, potholes, bad weather and possible dangers.

Then you have your backseat passengers *Subconscious Awareness* that includes: a child *the Inner Child*, an angry teenager, *the Inner Teenager,* a set of parents*, the Parental Awareness*, a few siblings, *Familiar Awareness*, a set of grandparents, the elders*, Ancestral Awareness*, passed down by epigenetics, some pets, *Instinctual Awareness*, a wide range of *Elemental and Natural Awareness*, and social constructs, *Social Awareness*.

The elders, always look out the window, giving advice when they see fit, but not nearly as much information as they would if had visited with them or asked them questions. Some elders are louder, causing much fighting with the child and the teenager, the navigator, and the driver. They hold keys to your generational gifts, culture, traumas, curses, medicine and ancestral wounds. The ancestral maternal energies are held in front of the pelvis and the womb, while ancestral paternal energies are held behind the pelvis and the lower back.

The parents, are the mother and father energies, the duality of the divine feminine and divine masculine, which reside in your internal world. They generally give you the roadmap, but it's up to you to parent your inner child, inner teenager, and siblings. They set the stage and teach you what they've learned from their elders. The deep seeded mother and father wounds reside in these energies. They may or may not reflect the light, and they have a lot of *"I told you so,"* moments. Sometimes they are gentle mirrors, and other times they are as harsh as the elements. They hold the keys to your ability to parent your inner child and teen, as well as how you parent your own children.

The child, is creative, sweet, innocent, and full of joy and light; however, they can be easily bored, needing attention, stimulation, food, and potty breaks. Their chatter is near constant: *"Look at me! Look at me!"* They hold the keys to the astral world, dream world, Higher Self, Source, imagination, bliss, meditation, dreams, play and the *Eternal Now.*

Imagination holds the keys to your creations, potentials, and solutions. It holds the keys to your unordinary experience, to traverse the astral and spiritual realms and all expansive possibilities. You enter the realms through **Meditation State and Dream State of Consciousness.**

Meditation holds the keys to your tranquility and the ability to traverse the astral and spirit realms while awake; and through **Dream State** your body recovers from the physical world and you enter dream world. Both meditation and dreams state can be controlled if you hold focus, allowing you to exist anywhere at any time. However, without focus they can also be the cause of nightmares and chaos. This is why it is so important to cleanse, purge, ground, transmute, and know thyself.

The teenager, projects their frustrations, and argues with the elders, the parents, the siblings, and the child. They are very defensive. They hate being bored even more than the child does. The teenager throws their energy around, louder than anyone else, always making a fuss about something and seeking a lot of external validation and stimulation. They hold the keys to your ego, divine rage, independence and justice.

The siblings, like the parents and elders, hold masculine and feminine energies. They help you relate to what is familiar. They set the stage for how you relate to those who seem familiar. They can be gregarious or very judgmental. They can be harsh judges of character and reinforce the expectations of parents and elders. They are also your brother and sister wounds. These energies can be felt between the shoulder blades, root, sacral ,as solar plexus, heart and throat chakras. They hold the keys to your how you show up for yourself, for others and soul family.

The pets, offer support but need lots of walks, sustenance, and attention. There can be a variety of ways these animals present themselves. However, because of their nature, they are always on guard and alert until you learn to tame and befriend them. They can be fiercely nasty to any and all threats. They will most definitely chase and bite the hand that feeds them until you learn how to coexist. They hold the key to your instinctual, protection, primal and sexual energies.

The social constructs, represent all external programming and expectations: family, school, church, work, unspoken rules, time, etc. Each requires a different version of you to show up. These are the masks that become the most apparent. They hold the keys to your ability to network.

The elements, earth, wind, air, fire, lightning, and celestial bodies also have something to say, as well as ***nature, animals, bugs and plants.*** They are the oldest of your ancestors, grandparents and oldest siblings. They were here long before you were. They hold the keys to safety, shelter, food, water, medicine, and ancient wisdom, but you cannot hear them over the near-constant chatter, intrusive thoughts, doubt, and the overwhelming drain from the modern world that bombards your senses.

The 5th Phase: Observer Awareness

Now, imagine you are driving along a mountainside on a dewy foggy night, with only fog lights to aid you. You have no idea there is a storm ahead because you are not fully aware of your internal world, narrowing the scope of your external world. You are blinded by a veil made up of many masks. Your vision is narrowed and short-sighted. Now you're in quite the predicament, with accidents just around the corner.

The elders, elements, and pets are all allies, but you haven't had the quiet mind to take in what they have to share, nor do you ask, so they let you drive haphazardly. They cannot interfere with your *Free Will*. However, they will take hold of the wheel when you are not able to, and in doing so, it can be very chaotic when all the energies feel they should be the driver. As you know, a ship can only have one captain at the helm.

The driver, the front seat passenger, the child, the teenager, the parents, and the elders are all subconscious shadow versions of yourself. As you can see, the van is quite crowded, leaving very little room for you to attune to your dashboard, navigation system, radio, or higher self. Essentially, you are offline and ill-equipped.

Now, pan out, and you can see the van and all its internal functions and malfunctions. This is your ***Observer Awareness***. It is self-aware but stays mostly observant of all that is happening with the driver and passengers. Like the elders, elements, nature, and pets, if you do not invite them in, they can only observe. It holds the keys to discernment, foresight, precognition, and is the bridge between you, your higher self and Source.

They might see a tree in the road and urge the passengers to demand you stop and eat. Begrudgingly, you do so, averting an accident. You're not quite self-aware, but you're *safe-ish,* provided the shadows of your subconscious do not get spooked, yank the wheel, and drive you headfirst off a cliff.

Now, pan out further, and you are now the observer of the van, seeing other vans. This is your ***Higher Self.*** You can tune into these energies without being fully aware of the dynamics of your higher self, though you are far more acute and precise when you are fully aware of its presence. Your higher self holds the key to all your spiritual gifts and knowing.

The 6th Phase: Awareness of Your Auric Field

You begin to realize — or perhaps remember — that you have an aura, an energetic field that surrounds you and extends about 3 to 6 feet outside of your vessel and it can exceed further than your eyes can see. This is a sensation, not necessarily a visual experience at first, though it can be. As you become more attuned to the extension of your field, you also become more aware of other beings — like animals, insects, and plants — that share space with you.

It is not only outside of you but also enveloping you and your immense Light body. You discover that your Light serves as a powerful tool for navigating your vast internal world and physical body, as well as for aiding others. With focus, you can heal your own body and share your Light in a myriad of ways. This is the foundational work done by Reiki practitioners and other healers.

The 7th Phase: Awareness of Your Third Eye

You begin to reconnect with your body and develop a heightened awareness of your third eye. It starts as a subtle sensation, a tickle on the roof of your mouth, gradually rising toward your third eye and through your crown. As you focus on it, the sensation becomes more distinct, consistent and expansive. Over time, you will experience more frequent downloads, epiphanies, and moments of euphoria.

Your spiritual gifts will also become increasingly apparent, even if they are not yet fully online. As your awareness expands and your remembrance strengthens, so too will your gifts. During this process, maintaining good spiritual hygiene and grounding should be your primary focus.

The 8th Phase: Heightened Self Awareness

All four bodies are sensitive. You are still in reactive and survival mode, burning in your own hell, though you may not be fully aware of it yet. This is why you must come to know all that burns you — everything you mask, and the who, what, when, where, why, and how you mask. Some triggers need healing, while others are spiritual gifts trying to make themselves known. This is the point where you turn from merely acting out of woundedness, and the deconstruction of your self-concept begins: *Who are you?*

The 9th Phase: Self-Actualization

Just because you are aware of these states, you have yet to embody them. You must pull all these wisdoms into embodiment for the Rebirth to take place. This is where **Self-Actualization Awareness** begins. You start to ask yourself, *Who AM I? What AM I? Why AM I? Where AM I? How AM I?* A new definition emerges, with it, a shift in perspective and consciousness. There is no room for masks in these waters. For you will find the confinement of shallow waters suffocating.

Many times, when we are younger, we are naturally gifted, but then we reach a point where we forget. In the great forgetting, we become blind to our own divinity and the spiritual world. Once you cross a threshold beyond which there is no return, the quest for Remembrance begins; an undeniably long Journey to Self — *Self-Actualization.*

The 10th Phase: Know Thyself

There is a difference between concepts and embodiment. While every step may have been in your peripheral vision, it starts to converge and the process of your evolution is in the making while you are in the moments of living.

This is when it becomes clear that you must undertake the undaunting task of shadow work. This work requires time, attention, energy, focus, and grace. You will be called to address your inner child, inner teenager, mother, father, sibling, ancestral and generational wounds, triggers, attachments, betrayals, and projections. It will be deeply emotional at times.

In this phase, you become highly attuned to your thought processes — what is truly of you and what is not. You begin to understand how deeply projections have interfered with your ability to move in accordance with your spirit. You shift from automatic, repetitive states into a more self-aware consciousness and an intentional way of *be-ing*.

In this raw *hue-manness*, you begin to shed. You know you cannot turn back, for to do so would mean abandoning your spirit and your inner child to the chaos of your self-imposed hell — the one place only you have the power to free yourself from

Make no mistake, this is heavy work you are about to embark on. You will need to develop good spiritual practices that will aid in grounding, cleansing, purging, and transmuting your pain. Staying on top of spiritual hygiene practices is essential. As you strengthen your spiritual body so will the rest of your bodies.
— *As above, so below. As within, so without.*

In due time, you will befriend your shadows. You will come to understand that the masks you wore were once your fiercest protectors of your inner child. However, they can no longer be the ones driving your vessel.

The 11th Phase: Death of Identity

The first ego death is not a death of your ego entirely, though it is the shattering of some of your masks — like saying goodbye to a lifelong friendship. You know it's for the best, but it still hurts. This grief will persist until you are ready to accept and let go. As you process the grief and release the energy stored in your bodies, you begin to feel lighter.

For each mask you wear, you must let go and mourn the version of yourself you no longer embody. What is often not discussed is just how emotionally, mentally, physically, and spiritually painful this process can be. It feels like labor — because it is laborious to rebirth yourself. This is not only an emotional labor but also a labor of the spirit. To bring forth what is within requires a deep commitment to your whole *be-ing* — to authenticity and empathy for yourself.

Authenticity is a beautiful thing. You are born knowing the Light, but through the absence of conscious mirrors and the weight of projections, you mask and forget. Rediscovering yourself is an immensely freeing experience; it is a homecoming. It sets the stage for what you will never return to.

You come to understand that masking has been the cause for so much pain and strife, and that embracing your authenticity will inevitably provoke the parasites within others. These parasites rise to the surface because they have not yet faced their own shadows. Do your best not to engage with such energies or accept their projections. These moments are reflections of where you no longer belong and a testament to how far you have come.

The 12th Phase: Rebirth In The Making

After trial and error, you start to figure out the dashboard, the radio and GPS. You begin tapping into your higher self. You realize everything has been pulling your attention, energy, and focus. You stop the van abruptly. In this realization, you start addressing the noisy passengers. You find that each state of these beings represents different levels of consciousness, and you've been led in circles because the driver isn't fully self-aware nor is it making conscious decisions or taking intentional actions. Meanwhile, your van needs maintenance, tires, and gas.

Eventually, you refuel the van, make repairs, and maybe even get new tires. **Rebirth** enters the picture. You deconstruct every fiber of your consciousness, accept, and let go of what does not serve you and integrate the fragmented parts that have gone missing. You attend to the child, the elders, and the pets first, realizing they all hold infinite wisdom you've been ignoring. Then you address the defensive teenager and discover their anger stems from injustice and being ignored while trying to protect you. Finally, you sit down with the shotgun rider and realize they're terrible at navigating. Together, you study the dashboard, GPS, and radio. There is great wisdoms to share, and you are now obligated to heed their warnings. For you are no longer blinded by the veil of smoke and mirrors, and to ignore the elders would be walking with apathy.

The 13th Phase: Resurrection

Rebirth is quite like labor, with highs and lows and at some point, utterly painful. For every expansion, there is a contraction. You grieve, process, and make amends with all illusions that took you away from your sweeter self. You now know who you are and who you are not. Your ego shatters, an ego death if you will. You mourn for it all.

Like a phoenix rising from the ashes. Now you embark on your **Resurrection.** There is calm as you transition from subconscious to conscious awareness. In doing so, the dashboard, navigation system and radio start to harmonize. Now, you can feel and hear your higher self, and Source. While prayers are amplified with your voice, there is no need to speak because they are you, and you begin to commune with all the consciousness that resides in you. You will find you experience physical strength, there is a weightlessness in your body, and you gain speed into your steps. While your sword and shield are always there to protect, you are not as guarded as it once was.

The 14th Phase: Christ Consciousness

In the communion with your higher self, Source and self-actualization, and rebirth, **Christ Consciousness** becomes more than thought. You experience empathy for all that is you and all that surrounds you. You come to know and commune with all *be-ings, hue-man* and non-human. In the depths of you and your empathy, you discover you have the ability to heal.

Apathy will go against every fiber of your *be-ing. A*s you know *Empathy is Key* to it all. *The Kingdom of Heaven is Within You,* and you have a choice to reside in absolute empathy and bliss, or you can torment ourselves until the end of time. *Free Will is the Muscle of Choice*, so you must choose your Light. You come to *inner-stand* why the Creator cannot be the authority nor can it dictate your actions and therefore no one person can either; in doing so it would strip you of your *Free Will and Light*, both of which are our greatest gifts from the Creator, aside from empathy and your vessel.

This doesn't mean you won't have dangers along the way, nor can you avoid accidents entirely. You still must learn to listen to the elements, plants, animals, and others prone to veering off the road, as they lack spatial awareness, foresight, and operate subconsciously just as you once did. You embark on a new journey all together. One so foreign to what you have come to know up until this point.

The road is most certainly full of potholes. As you get better at using your GPS and antenna, your scope of sight and peripheral vision expands, and you gain not only foresight, but also the ability to see what others cannot — in both their surroundings and themselves.

You will learn that sometimes it is easier to journey a path less traveled. You do not have to do what others do. Your *Free Will* becomes undeniable. You fall in love with your van, your passengers, and your sovereignty. Now, you must maintain it all — *it's yours, all yours.* There is something undeniably glorious about belonging to yourself.

Now you move with excitement, embracing all that you are and all you have yet to discover. A new adventure awaits. You do not know where you are headed, only that you are called to follow your North node, and you can't help but answer the call, embracing every fiber of your *be-ing.*

The 15th Phase: Awakening of The Snake

A surge of energy flows from the root chakra all the way through to the crown chakra. Your root chakra feels full, as do all the other chakras, while your third eye and crown chakra begin to expand into a sensation of fullness — moving from a pinpoint to about 2 to 3 inches in diameter — and the back and neck release some of their stored tension.

This intense and charged energy can be felt throughout your entire body. It is sensual and euphoric. Sensuality is more than just eroticism; it means that all the senses are heightened and experienced in a multi-dimensional way. It is merely a glimpse of how you will experience your world moving forward from the mundane to the extra ordinary. Channels, downloads, epiphanies, and visions will become more apparent.

Focus on your grounding during this time. It is very easy to get stuck in the eroticism and lose momentum, losing a sense of foresight. Your spiritual quest can lead you down the path of grand escapism. This can invite trickster spirits and spiritual attacks and can result in spiritual psychosis if you are not grounded. Conserve your essence to the best of your ability.

Though for some, this is induced by years of meditation, for myself this was a spontaneous event, brought on by grief and a determination to feel whole again. In my mind's eye, I saw two black snakes crisscrossing through my body and bursting through my crown, turning into one massive snake that resembled an anaconda. Many refer to this as a Kundalini Awakening. At the time, I had not yet heard the term.

So much poured through me. I saw myself in the mirror and realized that I hadn't been looking at myself with the same loving eyes that I looked at my children with. I was a stranger to myself. I realized I hadn't truly looked myself in the eyes in years, probably never. Here I was, in my late 30s, and I had barely noticed myself for a very long time. I had reached a point in my life where I felt like I was absolutely nothing — literally nothing, to no one, not even myself. It couldn't have been further from the truth, but a lifetime of staring into those with black eyes and believing their lies had distorted my self-perception. I realized I had believed the lies, gaslighting and false programming.

How my heart broke into a million pieces. I realized I wasn't as awful, dumb or as ugly as I had been treated. I wasn't the ugly duckling I thought I was, but a swan who could not see herself. The outpouring of emotions when I realized I had broken my own heart. I soon realized that this was probably the greatest of all my sins. For I had not even believed in my own experiences, thus denying my existence — and in turn, denying the existence of my own divinity and the Creator.

In those moments of great unraveling, I decided that I would commit to my healing and spirituality once and for all. I would look at myself and treat myself as I would an infant. Even if I had to talk to myself like a child to make sure I was not ignoring my needs.

The longest journey I have ever known is from the head to the heart — to know thyself. The divine union and marriage between my vessel and higher self. For the spirit is always evolving, abundant, infinite, elusive, and hidden in plain sight.

The 16th Phase: Walking Back the Soul

Soul loss happens for a many of reasons and is the cause of a variety of *dis-eases*. As you face each wound, it becomes an act of deconstructing all that you are and how you've come to be. The energies of these wounds will slowly release, making room for the Light to return. This deconstruction is also an unraveling of your energy and everything that has distorted and bound you. Your body cannot withstand both forces at once, and the spirit, being sweet and pure, is not meant to endure constant pain.

It is easy to experience soul loss if you are perpetually in a state of anxiety, fear, anger, or guilt. These are the parasites that devour your essence from the inside out. You become your own diligent surgeon. To be your own healer, you must pay close attention, focus, and use your Light in a way that clears you of all that binds you. Yes, healers can guide you, but ultimately, you must learn to do this yourself and maintain your spirit.

In due time, your reconnection to Source will strengthen. Your Light will not only return — it will grow exponentially. You will find that the world around you is far more magical than you ever thought possible.

The 17th Phase: Magnetism

This can be an exciting phase. There are no coincidences, only synchronicities. That which resonates with you will draw your truths to you. It will also draw those who are attracted to your light and perhaps there is a need. This doesn't mean that parasitic energies resonate with your *be-ing,* but there is an affinity for it. You will attract all manners of energy — anything from animals, bugs, children, those who have passed, to accidents, near-misses, and vampiric energies in public.

When you are not fully grounded and your boundaries are not strong, it can become overwhelming. It takes time to get the hang of walking with magnetism. Knowing your triggers, developing good self-care rituals, grounding, setting healthy boundaries, and holding yourself accountable, is essential. Once you make an agreement with yourself, you must adhere to it to the best of your abilities. Do not allow yourself to become too rigid. As you evolve, so does everything around you — even some of the agreements you once made with yourself. Stay open to growth and the fluidity of your journey.

Magnetism will attract many who need your light. Be mindful, that some lessons are not for you to learn firsthand, merely what *not* to do. If you stay where you do not belong, you will get burned and you will be forced to face another lesson similar to the one you did not learn from and perhaps another tower moment.

The consequences of standing in your truth will attract and repel equally. Learn to accept, let some situations be, let go and just observe. Try not to attach yourself to situations that do not serve your highest potential.

The 18th Phase: Discernment

Discernment is the ability to perceive and understand things clearly, especially when it comes to distinguishing between what is true or false, beneficial or harmful, aligned with your higher self or misaligned. It involves a deep sense of awareness, intuition, and wisdom, allowing you to make decisions that honor your spirit. Avoiding the hard lessons and possible tower moments. Unfortunately, wisdom comes by way of lived experiences of the hard lessons, but only if you learned them well.

It goes beyond surface-level judgments, enabling you to see the underlying energies and motivations behind situations, people, or choices. Discernment requires both patience and openness, allowing you to tune into subtle messages and trust your inner knowing without being swayed by external pressures or distractions.

The 19th Phase: Spiritual Gifts

Your spiritual gifts will become more attuned, and your connections will become more apparent. Like crawling, everything you have learned up until now was but the beginning. As you progress, everything will expand at a faster rate and your spiritual gifts become accessible to you with ease.

As your ability to hold focus improves, you will begin to feel an expansion in your third eye. With focus, all of your senses become heightened, and your peripheral vision expands. You'll notice the energy bodies of people, places, things, and all life more clearly.

Time will slow down in your reality, allowing you to observe even the smallest movements. When you burn incense and hold focus, the smoke will rise straight up. With continued practice, you'll be able to sustain this focused state longer, and your prayers will become more coherent, and potent. You may even experience spontaneous healing from lifelong diseases during these moments.

The 20th Phase: The Jaguar

Pan out even further, and you see miles around — other vehicles operating with no self-awareness or consciousness. Like a jaguar, fully aware of itself, it is the observer of observers, observing others. Almost everything is curious and fascinating to study the existence of your own *be-ing* and that of the external world outside you. It can see the energies, egos, tricksters, parasites, shadows, and masks.

You also realize that you wield a great power to be this observant and could also do harm, there for you must honor and respect the space and *Free Will* of another. In that way you protect them from your own internal hell and projections that you are emerging from.

The 21st Phase: The I AM

This is a spectacular moment in your journey. It is the moment when you can see the fractal of life and its infinite mirrors — *The Great I AM.*

The Great I AM is more intelligent and self-aware than all the other states of awareness. Though it does not make you fully aware until you are ready, this is also where you bring forth your Light to the parts of you that need healing and will do so with ease, even without your awareness. It has no sense of time and cares not for the physical world. It runs purely off of divine timing.

You come to realize that you are of the same Light as Source, and that we are all mirrors of Source and of each other. You become acutely aware of *all* your aspects — your shadows, your higher self, your observer, the observer of the observer, and the observer of the observer of those outside of you. You are not who they say you are. You are who you think and say you are. This is not just a declaration of self. This is a pivotal moment when you know you are a child of the divine. You are divinity, making itself *known* and observing itself.

In this expanded awareness, you can see the veil clouding their sight and their personal hell. You come to understand that we are indeed our own worlds, and there is a burning sensation as the veil is dense and heavy. You become attuned to your own energies and learn to discern the entities around you for what they truly are. You also learn to disengage from energy vampires and their parasites, choosing not to engage with that which seeks to drain your essence.

The 22nd Phase: Bound

You have already done so much work up to this point, addressing the obvious wounds: your inner child, inner teenager, mother, father, sibling dynamics, ancestral and generational wounds, projections, and betrayals. Much of this has been at the core, but these are not the roots. The roots are stored deep within your energetic body.

You begin to physically feel chains binding your entire *be-ing*. These chains burn and can be felt in the back, neck, arms, and legs. It feels as if you have been weighed down, both literally and figuratively. When they finally break, there will be an outburst of emotional, physical, mental, and spiritual energy. A mixture of anger, bliss, euphoria, tears, hysterical laughter, downloads, and epiphanies will surge through you. The experience is exhilarating, as much of the pain will dissipate.

You will come to realize that rebirth feels very much like labor. With every contraction, there is expansion, and with every expansion, there is contraction. When you come down from this energetic high, you will need to process and integrate the experience. Keep your focus on grounding, cleansing, purging, and transmuting — it will serve you well.

The 23rd Phase: Shattering of Swords

This feels like swords in your back, shoulder blades, neck, base of your neck, top of your skull, third eye, and throat chakra. You may experience extreme pain, unable to move, only to have the sword shatter in an instant, and with it, the pain disappears. These are the wounds of betrayal — either from yourself, from those close to you, or from both. Again, this will be accompanied by bursts of emotional, mental, physical, and spiritual energy as before. But this time, you are well equipped with spiritual tools and it is not as exhausting as before.

Instead of blood, energy pours out. This can be emotionally draining, and you must focus your light on these wounds to heal them. All wounds heal from the inside out, so it may take time for the energy to stop flowing. During these times, you can easily become fatigued. Do your best not to engage with anything or anyone that drains you.

This happened after I faced familiar betrayal and ancestral trauma, after I had moved much of the energy out of my body. I hadn't realized I was being spiritually attacked in such a way, but this moment confirmed my suspicions. Spiritual baths, Limpias, clean eating, plenty of water, lighting copal, focusing my Light on those wounds, and going deep within to call forth my ancestors to heal these wounds became my focus.

The 24th Phase: Bursting the Chrysalis

There is immense energy and strength that comes with this initial breakthrough. It is like a butterfly bursting through its chrysalis. It feels as if wings are emerging from your back — electric, euphoric, and liberating. It is as though you are moving freely for the first time. You can physically feel the difference between the veil and the hell that others are trapped in. The veil can be experienced through all your senses. You can see it, hear it, smell it, feel it, and taste it. It is heavy, and it utterly burns.

You have come to know that we are truly our own worlds. You come to understand why others mask and are not aware that they are burning, and they are burning others. You shift from perceiving to knowing that Heaven or Hell is not outside of you. Both can be experienced, and you absolutely have a choice, as *Free Will* and Empathy are your birthrights.

You also understand why *you* cannot interfere with another's Free Will, and why the Creator cannot interject. *Free Will is the*

225

Muscle of Choice. You must choose it for yourself, as there is no freedom without choice.

Your insights sharpen, and you begin to see situations as lessons and opportunities for growth — not as experiences of suffering. You move from perceiving the illusions of the veil, to *innerstanding* how masks and projections clouded your vision, creating so many false narratives and realities.

This is also a very emotional period. Just as a butterfly emerges, its wings are not yet solid. They are wet and require time to strengthen. Similarly, you are "goopy," with an overflow of energy. You may find yourself sharing more than you usually would. Be very mindful of who you share with, as you will be particularly sensitive during this time. You are an Angelic sacred infant of the divine, and you must treat yourself as such.

The 25th Phase: Naked

You and your wings feel bare, as if shackled, with chains hooking into specific points of your wings. You will need to allow yourself to purge, to rid your vessel of the pains that weigh you down. This will create space for the Light to return.

Energetically, it feels as though you are naked — battered and bloodied — and energy pours out from every wound caused by the chains and swords. This is a very tender part of your journey. Masking becomes more painful than allowing others to see the Light you once hid. You are incredibly vulnerable in this state.

The 26th Phase: Shattered Shackles

The shackles in your wings shatter, but where they were once chained, it now feels like gaping bullet wounds. Not as severe as the set of swords, but energy does leak from these spots, and you must heal them. These were ancestral, generational curses — mindsets that held you and your family back.

While you may have understood this concept intellectually before, it is now becoming a tangible experience. Concepts transform into lived experiences, and experiences turn into lessons. Lessons evolve into knowing, and knowing becomes wisdom. Wisdom then shapes a way of *be-ing*. There is a rinse-and-repeat cycle until the energies are fully understood, learned, and integrated.

You begin to realize that some of these weights were not of your own doing, but they are your responsibility to break and heal — for yourself, your children, and those around you. You take on the heavy task of being the generational curse breaker and a lighthouse for others.

The 27th Phase: The Rainbow Fish

Your wings feel more skeletal than full — some feathers remain, but they are sparse. You will be extremely raw. Like the rainbow fish, you come to understand that it wasn't just others who plucked out your feathers, but you did too. You become acutely aware of the self-inflicted damage. You realize that much of your suffering was caused by your own doing. By breaking your own heart and not fully believing in your experiences — therefore, you are unable to fully believe in your existence. These are the

227

greatest sins you can commit against yourself, as you inherently deny your own Light.

You must focus on healing all those wounds, detaching from those who once hurt you, and realizing you cannot burn yourself alive for others who are not yet ready. It is time to call your energy back.

The 28th Phase: Regrowth

One by one your feathers begin to grow back. You gain physical strength and endurance, and how others perceive you begins to align more closely with how you see yourself.

Forgiveness becomes effortless. While challenges may still arise, your body no longer holds onto the pains of the past. A sense of acceptance emerges, allowing things to be as they are.

You start to walk on water — your consciousness has elevated to a level where you can move swiftly through crowds, avoiding the chaos and nightmares of others if you so choose. Your energy field and spiritual gifts start to crystalize, and you can now offer your Light freely, without needing to dim or drain your own.

The 29th Phase: Solidified

You master belief and faith, beginning the process of mastering your energies and gifts. It becomes more challenging for others to knock you off your footing, and you feel less drained by their energy.

You are able to hold your boundaries firmly yet gracefully, without expending unnecessary energy. While your masks, sword, and shield remain available, they no longer feel necessary. You find greater security and protection in having fully accepted both your shadows and your Light.

A near-constant connection to Earth Mother and Source, anchors you. You become intentional with your actions, thoughts, and words. Your ability to heal both yourself and others becomes potent, radiating strength and clarity.

The 30th Phase: Embodiment

This phase is about learning to walk in balance — to be a *Hue-man;* to be both Light and Matter. You become the walking embodiment of Empathy, Grace and Miracles. You are here to aid, heal, teach, and uplift, while also observing the hells of this world without getting lost to the madness.

There is no turning back from this journey. You can't unsee the proof of your existence, experiences, and gifts. You are Divinity — *Creation making itself known.*

This phase can be emotional as you come to *inner-stand* that we indeed are our own worlds, and not everyone is meant to be within your orbit. It is not easy to walk with sight when so many others wear blinders. But you must remain on your path and purpose, holding yourself with the same reverence as an infant. This is a new way of *be-ing* — *A Rebirth and Embodiment.*

The 31st Phase: Forgiveness, Trust, and Surrender

Much of my anger and rage in my youth was because I didn't realize that empathy and apathy were two very different languages, experiences and worlds. Those who walk with apathy cannot hear the plights of those who are suffering. And those who walk with empathy burn just by listening to those who speak false truths. They are two completely different realities. Like children, they know not what they do.

I will not deny that forgiveness has always been an elusive concept to me, prior to my re-awakening. I understand the intense struggle to forgive, however when you do so, you free your body of any unnecessary tension. The release is euphoric in nature as you are no longer chained by the once-was.

Forgiveness should not cover up misdeeds or force you to stay where you do not belong. Once someone shows you the *"worst time,"* you are only hurting yourself if you entertain more than your capacity. Learning to know your own limits and setting boundaries will quicken your healing time.

When you truly trust yourself, you can trust others. This is why you must know thyself. Accepting the truth, even if they may sting, reject, or create false projections. Respecting space allows for trust to strengthen, and respect is bare minimum. Trust is vital for any relationship you form, whether it is platonic or romantic. Trust is something that must be earned, cultivated and protected.

The 32nd Phase: Surrender to the Is-ness

By now, you have come to know your passions, your principles, your light, your gifts, and your creativity. You are not weighed down by the past, for you are rooted in the *Is-ness* of the *Eternal Now*. In this state, you walk in your truths, for to deny them is to deny your very existence. You are infinitely unfolding, and your potential is limitless. How you move is between you and Creator, as you are no longer bound by the illusions of the *once-was*.

In trusting yourself, your experiences, and your beliefs, you surrender your sword and shield. While they are there, it is unnecessary because you have faith in yourself and make amends with all that has transpired and all that is. It does not mean you're weak or you should not use your voice. It simply means you are no longer burning and choose peace, kindness, empathy, grace, unconditional love and radical acceptance where possible.

The eternal heaven becomes solidified. That these moments here with our Earth Mother, is the vacation from Eternity. While you have a choice, you also cannot entertain the hells of the past, or the hells of another nor can you be the cause of harm. In many ways, you are limited because. — *for now, you are knowing.*

While you may choose not to use your gifts, they are not meant solely for you alone. They are to be of Service to Others — good children to our Earth Mother, and good brothers and sisters to one another and all the *be-ings*.

Chapter 12: Living in Ceremony

"Clearing the Smoke Between Worlds" ©*Zoila Luz Rosario Masiak 2024*

Living your Life in Ceremony nurtures your spiritual body, strengthens your spiritual gifts as well as your physical body. When you invoke the power of intention into your life, you will find that most tasks done with intention add to the overall relief. Rituals that you create for yourself hold more weight. Always start with a clear mind, holding good intentions and gratitude, when you call forth any element or spirit you wish to honor.

We are like a blade of grass, energies are always flowing in and flowing out. You will need to create a rituals; introducing yourself, grounding, good spiritual hygiene, and pulling the energies into and out of you. Creating and preforming routine rituals for yourself will calm all four bodies and quicken your connection and healing time. When times are rough, you will have measures in place to both cope and move the dense energies out. Letting dense energies settle into the body will create rigidity. To bring forth your higher self and to co-create you will need to maintain flow, and you this by treating yourself and the world around you like it is sacred. When you realize your own Divinity, you will come to understand the Divinity of All Life that surrounds you. You will find that you will walk and move with gentleness and purpose. You become a *Walking Ceremony* with every step you take.

Make a point to stay grateful. Give thanks to the Creator, your breath, and your time. Give gratitude to those around you. It will aid in keeping you in the now. Every moment of your Life spent in motion or silence is an opportunity to give gratitude and set your intentions for your actions. This is what it means to live your Life in Ceremony. Call in your ancestors with offerings by lighting candles, incense, or smoke cleanse. Lift their spirits with gratitude and speak to them like any beloved grandparents. Feast the Spirits as often as possible. Watch and listen to the synchronicities. Their soft whispers remind us of their presence.

Make space for intentional prayer and meditation. Allow enough time for silence. It is in the in-betweens that you hear the whispers of grace, truth, and wisdom. Frequent and rigorous spiritual cleansing: ceremonial baths, feasting the spirits, energy healings, Limpias, and smoke cleansings; will aid in keeping those dreams close and the nightmares at bay. Seek council and Elders when there is a need for support and never be ashamed of such requests. Those who walk freely of spiritual narcissism will offer support without being asked. They will feel you and make their presence known.

Love yourself as if you would love any child. Above all, give yourself grace. For that is what is needed and is required. Forgive yourself for what you did not know. You don't know what you don't know, and that applies to your external world and inner world. When you forgive, you set your mind and soul free. *–forgiveness, it does a body good.*

Forgiveness is not just one mindful thought or action; it takes time to deconstruct, understand and integrate. Don't rush the process. It will come as you choose grace. You do this to set your soul free, to break the chains that bind; and when you do the work, you break them for others. Simultaneously, forgiveness does not mean you are required to let the ones who burn you, burn you again. Like Service to Others, forgiveness has been weaponized.

Healing Tips

Healing is not linear, and most certainly not singular. Give yourself adequate time to digest, process and integrate. Here are a few healing tips you can incorporate into your life to aid you in your journey and uplift your spirit. Remember, healing is a journey — be patient with yourself and trust the process.

3-6-9 Method

Nikola Tesla's "369 theory" suggests that the numbers 3, 6, and 9 hold significant meaning and are interconnected, representing the fundamental principles of the universe. The 3-6-9 Method and The Law of Attraction are frequently used for manifestation; it may be applied to your overall health as well. Speaking to your body first with the mind, then with intentional thoughts, then with your voice will aid in your recovery time. This is where the power of prayer can be most potent to your personal needs. When you apply it to healing, you will speak your intentions to your body 3 times a day. Repeat your mantra or prayer: 3 times in the morning, 6 times in the afternoon, and 9 times before bed.

Affirmations

Affirmations are positive statements or phrases that individuals repeat to themselves with the intention of fostering a positive mindset, self-esteem, and personal development. The idea behind affirmations is rooted in the concept that the thoughts you consistently focus on can shape your beliefs and influence your actions. By repeating positive affirmations regularly, you will have the power to reprogram, drown out the parasites that have wormed their way into your subconscious mind and will cultivate a more optimistic and empowered outlook on life.

Affirmations will aid in your manifestations as well. Here are a few affirmations that I use:

"I am a child of the Sun. I am healthy. I am protected. I am loved and I am deserving of the love that I give."

"I am the answer to my ancestor's prayers. I am abundant in spirit. I am who I say I am. I am the light."

"I am infinite potential. I am creation. Each day, I attract opportunities that elevate my life."

"I am magical. Each day, I will dream, and from my dreams I will create a reality filled with love and abundance."

"I am the walking embodiment of Grace and Miracles."

Ancestral Healing

Addressing your ancestral healing can be very dense and heavy work. This honestly, has been the heaviest of my chains. It is not easy to address 100 or 1000 years in intergenerational trauma. The deeper you go in your healing, the more you will be confronted with the past and called to break your chains fully. This means you will eventually come face to face with the dark history of your ancestors.

Either Colonized or Colonizer; both sides will make themselves known and you will be comforted with dark truths. The further you go down this path, you will find that Our Earth Mother calls to us all, and there you will be called to sacrifice your colonized mind. You will realize the apathy spirits and the colonizer spirit, which is the reason why you suffer and all around you suffer as well.

Some ancestors are your greatest allies while others are your greatest adversaries, and they do not like anyone. Especially if you are going against the grain. It is important to know them well because they will hide in the most unassuming ways. You will need to sit with them for a while until you know their energies as they may pull you off course. As an elder once told me, *"No one has a right to dictate your spirit, not even your ancestors."* That simple line freed me from the ancestral colonizer energies that been holding me back for so long. May they liberate you, as they have liberated me.

Start with the lineage of your grandmothers and grandfathers first. This will narrow your focus. Find healers who have done the work. They will be able to help deconstruct.

Alternative Healers

Consider seeking a healer. The range of alternative healers can be vast, such as energy healers, elders, light workers, reiki practitioners, shamans, and others from various cultural backgrounds. These individuals will get the ball moving. There is a plethora of alternative healers and energy workers who are here to assist in *the Great Mass Awakening.*

Alternative healers benefit the whole, as you are not just a physical body. These healers will aid you in ways that you can best assist yourself and reflect unconditional love and acceptance. When choosing a healer, choose one that resonates with your

Spirit. A healer cannot maintain your homeostasis for you; that is contingent on your own *Free Will*. You must stay on top of your grounding and spiritual hygiene.

Breath Work

Breath is the vital force that sustains life, a gift from the Creator. It carries the vitality of our higher self, bringing forth our subconscious to the conscious. It is our interconnectedness with all living beings and the cosmos. Our breath is the bridge between the physical and spiritual realms, the connection to the greater universe above and equally infinite within. Breath work is key to maintaining your essence, as it is your breath that carries the spirit of you.

Breathing adequately from the diaphragm will help strengthen your core and ability to maintain your energy and emotions. Breath work such as somatic breathing, allows you to control emotions in times of significant obstacles and oppositions. With practice, breathwork helps slow down enough to have a clear line of sight and the ability to manipulate your perception of time, giving way to your potential for creation.

You will have better control of your vagus nerve. "The vagus nerve represents the main component of the parasympathetic nervous system, which oversees a vast array of crucial bodily functions, including control of mood, immune response, digestion, and heart rate." (National Library of Medicine)

Learning to breathe from the diaphragm during the appropriate times saves a lot of your breath. Do not waste your breath on anyone committed to not hearing you. It is okay to walk away. Do not let guilt hinder you, for not making space for those who wish you ill.

Shallow breathing will help regulate your nervous system and cardiovascular system; however, loss of breath for too long causes a loss of essence. You want to breathe shallowly in the presence of a vampire. It allows you not to lose your breath in their company. And if need be, the energy to leave a situation if an exit is presented as an option.

When you begin to stand in your power, you become an immovable object with our feet deeply rooted in the earth. With enough practice, you learn not to waste your breath on others, committed to their parasites and vampiric ways.

Calling the Soul Back

"Calling back the soul" typically refers to shamanic practice where individuals seek to recover or reintegrate fragmented aspects of their soul that have become disconnected due to various traumas. Anything or anyone who calls forth remembrance of our sweeter selves, has the most potency. In those moments you can return to innocence, and you can choose to walk with your infinite wisdom as you once did as a child. Sometimes you can have spontaneous moments. Other times you need assistance from healers to hold your hand, call forth, and walk with you during transition and metamorphosis.

Calling back your soul can be done by yourself; it also can be undaunting. If you are struggling, find a healer who can assist in calling back your soul. Having a healer or two that you can ask questions can help quicken your healing time.

As your purge, your vessel will feel free, allowing for the Light to return, a tempering of the soul occurs. There is a near constant flow state, of creating, observing, learning, and letting go. Stay diligent with your spiritual hygiene and grounding practices. Over time they become wonderful tools to bring you back to a space of peace when the waters are rough. Listen to music that brought you the most joy as a child, the songs that lifted you up. Do as artist do and create. It doesn't have to be perfect, just that you move the magic through.

Dance often, as it helps to move the energies and connect you to Source. Sing and rejoice because your breath is how your essence travels. Let your heart lead the way. With intent, moments of remembrance will flood in. Your job is to accept them and let them go.

Ceremonial Bathing

Ceremonial bathing is one of the easiest things you can do for yourself that allows for cleansing, flow, purging, and renewing of your energy and spiritual body. Incorporate ceremonial bathing into your life. It will aid in slowing down the speed at which you are thinking and lets in the natural flow and rhythm. Preparing for your bath in a sacred way creates a holy bond. It allows water to be treated like a sacred being she is, and you, too, are treating yourself like a sacred being.

Clean Eating

Eat as cleanly as possible. Nutritionally dense but low inflammation response foods, such as low sugar and mammal products, are optimal. Keeping your body healthy gives you energy when needed, making room to handle and cope with other unhealthy vampiric exposures. Everything has energy, and anything can give and receive energy. Growing your food and speaking loving thoughts and intentions will positively affect your body, heart, mind, and spirit. You will find what you eat does, in fact, taste better and will be more nutritionally dense when made with good intentions.

Cord Cutting

Imagine, if you will, the light body that your vessel contains has energy flowing from your vessels, it is made of billions of cosmic strings. These energy threads and cords allow us to perceive, see, and feel the world around us in a very deep and rooted way. These threads are everywhere, and anything can attach itself. Cord cutting is a practice that energetically cut ties between yourself and the influences outside of you.

Create

You are Creators and you Co-Create with the Creator, simply by being alive. The ingenious spark of creation and the ability to birth creations from your minds into reality is your magic. Creating is your most natural state, aside from breathing. Taking time in your life to create will teach you many lessons, aid in your ability to reach a flow state, and give you the confidence and independence that the mind needs to be fully sovereign. Create with a good heart and intent to uplift, and you will discover the creative genius within.

Declutter and Sweep

Make a habit of decluttering and throwing away what you do not use. Avoid letting dust pile up and that is also a visual representation of stuck energies. When you wipe down, sweep, or wash dishes, keep with the intent to clear energies. Living in Ceremony is a way of life.

Essential Oils

Essential oils have a wide variety of uses besides aromatherapy. Aromatherapy is beneficial. However, did you know that you can also cook with them, and use them for teas, baths, and massage? Some are antimicrobials while others are muscle relaxers or act as pain relievers, and some are vasoconstrictors or vasodilators.

They can be used in any way you need to heal yourself. Be cautious, as they are not all made the same, and some are cut with oils that are very caustic and will cause great damage to your eyes, gut, lungs, and skin.

Some are made ONLY for aromatherapy and absolutely should not be ingested. Others are made for topical uses or made to be ingested. Always do your research on the type of oils, what kinds of oils they are mixed with, their brands, and their uses and seek out an aromatherapist or herbalist who is well-versed before you ingest any essential oils. You will want to test a small spot on your skin, before adding it to food or bath to see whether you are not allergic.

Feast the Spirits

Take time to share a feast with your spirit guides, ancestors, and elements. These are small moments where you offer smudge, food, and drink to those you are honoring.

There are a variety of holy days that represent this idea throughout many cultures. Dia de Los Muertos, known for their colorful displays and parades, which is spent solely on feasting and honoring the ancestors. The days are spent in celebration of the Life and Death of those before us, remembrance of their stories, the resilience that brought us all here and all the favorite foods. Dia de los Muertos, to some, is seen as death worshiping, though that could not be further from its intentions. By celebrating death, you are honoring life and your fleeting time here before you return to the spirit world.

You will find that most of the Holy Days do precisely this. You acknowledge and honor what you love by sharing a meal with those you hold dear. In those moments, you give thanks to each other and the ones before you. Every creation that exists has a spirit. These are fundamental concepts in spirituality. In this way, every element, every creation can be and should be honored. When you feast the spirits on a regular basis, your connection with the spirits becomes stronger and with time, you will gain a lot of insights, and the epiphanies provide great relief and personal strength.

Fasting

Fasting is a practice in which individuals voluntarily abstain from consuming different types of activities, food, or drink. Fasting aids to detox and purify; the body and mind, enhance your connection with the divine, and gain greater insight or clarity.

Applying intermittent fasting to all aspects of your Life: activities, events, food, people, places, sexual activities etc. Spending time in your energy, with long breaks. You will learn to deconstruct your triggers and strengthen your capacity to handle said triggers with ease. Avoid or remove yourself from the presence of catalysts and triggers when possible.

Grounding

Grounding is a practice that involves connecting with the Earth's energy to balance and stabilize your own energy. It helps you become more centered, focused, and in tune with the present moment.

There are a variety of ways to get to the ground. Energetically speaking, grounding balances the 4 bodies' energies that are your vessel by connecting us to the earth. Getting a good grip on the grounding will conserve your essence and share with Our Mother. It also aids in the structure of your spiritual body, giving way to resilience in your physical body.

Grounding Allows spiritual abilities to strengthen, like Astral projection, discernment, precognition, recognition, transmuting, and so much more. Grounding is the most vital and fundamental to any spiritual practice. You can do this anywhere your vessel resides.

Herbalism

Like essential oils, there are a great number of herbs you must come to know and understand. Sacred herbs have multiple purposes and serve as antifungals and antimicrobials. This is why they are sacred; they can be used in a variety of ways besides clearing negative energies. Some are very toxic, so like anything else, research and seek out counsel from an herbalist before use. Local apothecaries are excellent places to find such healers who have spent their lifetime dedicated to plant medicines.

Massage Therapist or Chiropractor

A massage therapist or chiropractor will significantly help with neck and back pains. Back and neck misalignment causes disruptions in the CSF flow; it will cause increased headaches and even CSF leaks. Tension is often stored in the neck and back as well as betrayal. Keeping these muscles and joints relaxed aids the overall healing and reduces recovery time. Spiritual gifts may even strengthen when the back and neck are free from disruptions.

Medicine Wheel

Like anything else that is Native, be mindful and respectful. The Medicine Wheel is wildly different from people to people, depending on the culture, language, history, locations and differences between sacred animal and plant medicines.

Make sure you are doing your research and supporting Native peoples. Listen to them. There is a lot of pain for the First Nations people, and when you listen in, it will aid in your deconstruction and healing. Don't run from the pain that bubbles up from their truths. Like the buffalo, head it face-on, as that is the only way through the storm.

While I was not raised with culture, I have found the Medicine Wheel serves more than contemplation purposes. The Medicine Wheel contains a vast amount of information in such a simple symbol. It serves as an internal and external compass, knowledge of the seasons, migrations, North star, sunrise and sunset, a confirmation of what we know to be the circle of life and more.

It has been an aid to help me understand the importance of each direction. As you cannot argue with how the Sun rises and falls on us all the same

Media

Media and those who control the media are the driving force for a lot of the anger, anxiety, and the grooming our society. This also means keeping your media diet clean. Recognizing the problem and doing what you can to clean up the trash in your digital life.

Music that you listened to as a child or as a teenager that uplifted you, has the potential to aid in your return. It can invoke memories of happier times. While it can be emotional to review, you will find that what called in your sweet self then will uplift you today.

Be mindful of what you are listening to, playing, or watching. These energies are very intrusive. Anything that has the potential to create nightmares, you should limit. Yes, that even means the midnight snacks, games, movies, and music everyone is into. If the words do not sit well in your Spirit, avoid them altogether.

Meditation & Prayer

Meditation involves focusing the mind and minimizing distractions to achieve a state of mental clarity, relaxation, and heightened awareness. It is a fundamental skill that you must acquire to achieve self mastery. Meditation can be sitting still or in action such as doing dishes, dancing, singing, or painting. You do not have to sit for hours to reach nirvana. While sitting does help calm down the body for much needed rest. To *BE* alive is an action, so anywhere you choose to have a quiet, reflective mind, meditation is possible.

Make sure you have a firm grasp on grounding, as it is the basis and most important. It is easy to get lost in the sauce without it. Incorporate meditation and mindfulness, as it will aid in your spiritual growth and spiritual strength.

Mind Your Thoughts

As above, so below. As within, so without. Learning to focus your consciousness is a muscle that we are not often taught. Where your focus goes your attention goes. What you think, you believe. Your mind will manifest those beliefs into your reality. Minding your thoughts is not just to prevent you from thinking ill of others; it also keeps you from thinking ill about yourself. What you think is what you speak, and what you speak you will become. Staying observant of your internal dialogue will be beneficial for your growth, the ability to keep yourself safe and to manifest your dreams into reality.

Movement

To *be* alive is an action. Create, dance, sing, play, skip, etc. Whatever you do, move these energies through and out of your body as quickly as possible.

Dancing is one of my favorites and is a part of my everyday activity. Dance allows you to ground and transmute with our Earth Mother, while also allowing you to connect and flow with the Creator above. You cannot be possessed by too many intrusive thoughts and parasites if you are moving in flow.

Even if rocking in your chair is your only outlet. Give yourself permission and room to stem, as it helps regulate the ANS (autonomic nervous system) PNS (parasympathetic nervous system),and SNS (sympathetic nervous system)

When in public, make sure you do a lot of cardio and drink lots of water before you go out. Learning to breathe from the diaphragm during the appropriate times saves a lot of your breath. Keep your distance and breathe shallowly when you are in their presence. This should only be applied in short burst. Long periods of shallow breathing can cause its own complications.

Nature

Repeatedly, science backs up the positive effects of time spent in nature. Just like any *be-ing* in this world, you are a child of the Earth, Sun, Moon, Air, Water and Lightning. Like any animal, fungi, or plant, you will gain energy, guidance, knowledge, and wisdom from Source that gives and sustains life.

Make sure you are getting adequate time with Our Mother; the Sun, Our Father; the moon our Grandmother; and fresh air Our Grandfather. Speaking to the elements and other beings as if they are relatives, it calls forth honor and respect. It is a way to set intentions and reminds you to be good relatives to all that surrounds us.

Purge

Purging involves the releasing of pressure. When you need to purge, your body will involuntarily purge; It can be expressed through tears, shaking, laughter, gas, irritable bowel, sneezing or even through vomiting.

False attachments of parasitic energies create the smoke, diminishing your ability to feel and see clearly. Purging helps to maintain and manage the space your vessel needs to breathe fully. Once the emotions have been moved through, there will be relief and little recall unless it is purposely brought to the forefront of the mind. You become masters over your mind and, thus, your energies.

Let whatever emotions flow through. Emotions are Energy in motion. Let those feelings and thoughts come in, and let the tears flow out; eventually, the floodgates will burst, and they will burst forth with a deeper understanding of your internal universe and that outside of you. The epiphanies in these moments will be the keys that set you free. In doing so, you release all that was — making the lessons and Remembrance less harsh if faced again.

Rest

When you sleep, your spirits drift into the dream world, leaving your body to recuperate, heal, and grow. During these trips out, you have the capacity to control your dreams. If you go to sleep without calmness in your vessel, the potential for nightmares and night terrors increase.

People, places, or things that require sleep loss or disrupted sleep tend to have a lot of attachments and parasites. Summertime, with prolonged daylight hours, can induce mental stress. Simultaneously, long winter nights without the Sun can cause SADs (seasonal affective disorder), proof of the necessity of proper sun exposure and rest equally.

Getting the proper sleep is crucial to the overall health of your vessel. Extended periods of unrest will unravel the vessel. Rest is crucial for mind, body, emotions, and spiritual requirements.

With proper rest, you will be able to control your dreams. With enough practice, you will train the mind to lucid dreams. Your dreams will offer prophecies, solutions, and the ability to create, plan and prepare. Dreams also give you inner knowledge and personal strengths that will greatly improve your quality of life.

Shielding

Shielding takes grounding a step further. Shielding aids in your ability to stay grounded and present while also in movement. It is used to create a protective barrier around yourself, primarily through the use of intention and energy. This barrier is intended to safeguard against negative or harmful energies, emotions, or external influences, helping to maintain your emotional and energetic well-being. It is a way to maintain a sense of inner peace and clarity in the presence of potentially draining or disruptive energies. These techniques can include visualization, meditation, the use of crystals, affirmations, setting boundaries, and invoking the power of intention.

Smoke Cleanse

Smoke cleanse, more commonly known as smudging. When you include certain spiritual practices, like a smoke cleanse, you will begin to find the benefits are far greater than their initial uses. It is like a shower for your spiritual body. It breaks up negative energies and some herbs, like sage, act as anti-microbials.

Sacred herbs generally have multiple purposes besides smoke cleansing. They are considered sacred because they heal in a variety of ways. Some can be added to baths, food and teas as well, like bay leaf, eucalyptus, cinnamon, cooking sage, cedar, lemon grass, mints, rose, rue and more. Make sure you understand or consult an herbalist before you ingest any medicinal or sacred herbs. Preparation will vary depending on their usage.

White sage is endangered, due to the unethical cultivation at the hands of corporations or those who illegally enter sacred lands of Native peoples of the Southwest. Consider a more sustainable sage like cooking sage or prairie sage. Prairie sage is far more prolific. Consult and purchase from Native owned businesses, as they carry the ceremony and the traditions of sacred medicine.

The quality is generally superior, and it puts money directly into the hands of the very people who are the true land stewards.

Shadow Work

Shadow work refers to the process of exploring and integrating the darker or hidden aspects of your psyche and personality. It involves delving into your subconscious to uncover repressed emotions, past traumas, fears, generational trauma, and negative patterns of behavior. It aids in the discovery of the subconscious, healing, and, ultimately, the integration of the parts of the Spirit that may have escaped during a time of great fright also known as "soul loss."

Shadow work is a crucial step in achieving self-awareness, emotional well-being , radical self-acceptance and empathy for oneself. It involves introspection, therapy, and various self-help practices. By becoming active participants in your healing journey, shadow work allows for greater discernment. Allowing your mind the room to deconstruct and rebuild anew as many times as needed. It is how you learn and integrate the lessons that creates space to receive the gifts and to master those said gifts.

Holding yourself accountable for the waves of emotions gives you better control of your mind. It strengthens your discernment, as well as all the other gifts. It will clear the fog between the mirrors, freeing your mind of time, rather than spent on the toils and tribulations of the past.

Shadow work will cause a plethora of emotions to work through as well epiphanies and sometimes finding the divine comedy in it all. Remember, none of the nightmares can hurt you. If it causes physical pain, this is when you will need to express it the most. Let the floodgates open and purge. Let it out of all your bodies.

Identifying the *dis-ease* will heal you. You cannot heal what you do not acknowledge, know, or understand. The quicker you identify and understand, the quicker you can seek help or take the necessary actions to heal yourself. The quicker you release, the less you will store in your bodies.

Reflect on the nature of the situation in your life. Remove yourself from situations that make you feel uneasy or unsafe. Work on your generational trauma, direct and indirect traumas. The wisdom you find here is beyond space and time itself.

As you become more spiritual, you will find that Spirituality demands you to sacrifice that which makes you ill. It would be best if you decolonize and deconstruct your mind in every way. You will find much peace simply by not participating in the game of domestication and dogma.

Work through your shadow work; often, these are the grievances you have within yourself and with the world. Making agreements with yourself and keeping them gives you the strength to set firm boundaries for others. Remember, it is okay to feel your suffering was unjust, because it was. You were not supposed to suffer so. Avoid letting those feelings of grief settle into your bones.

Sobriety

All addictions have a potential for soul loss. Anything that inflames the body will also have the potential to inflame the ego. That is because the ego protects and guards the body when the spirit is not fully present, front line and center. When you are dealing with an addicted mind, you are dealing with irrational *being*. Not all addictions are substances. Many vampires are addicted to chaos. Even too much oxygen can steal your breath away.

One of the more widely acceptable substances abuse is alcohol. It has been promoted throughout the ages and has been the cause for unmeasurable amount of *hue-man* suffering. When you consider the history of alcohol and its widespread use, it truly is undaunting, and it is the cause for much of the intergenerational trauma.

It is no coincidence that alcohol has been referred to as "fire water" by some Native peoples. As it is an accelerant, disinfectant and burns the body when consumed. Alcohol consumption while pregnant leads to fetal alcohol syndrome. Alcohol is a depressant, not only in your mood, but also in your reaction time, a reduction in brain matter. It also calcifies your organs and pineal gland aka your third eye. Your pineal gland regulates your melatonin, which regulates your sleep. Without proper rest, you are vulnerable to nightmares, trickster spirits, parasites, spiritual attacks and overall collapse of the entire vessel and it's four bodies.

This happens because it dulls your intuitions and empathy, leaving holes in your energy field and causing soul loss. Alcohol is one of the quickest ways to lower your vibration and mental agility. Alcohol is used to extract the *essence* of a substance; your vessel and spirit are no different.

That being said, I will also include sacred herbs that are psychedelics in nature. While they have the power to connect and heal, dependency on them can invite trickster spirits if they are not honored and handled with great care. Spending too much time outside of your body compromises the reaction time needed to keep yourself safe. It leaves you open to potential spiritual bypassing and spiritual psychosis.

Journeying with the aid of sacred herbs is a valuable tool, but it comes with risks if boundaries are not respected. Just as those who perform the Sun Dance ceremonies do not remain suspended in such a state indefinitely, the same applies to Near-Death Experiences (NDEs) and shamanic journeying. While we possess the capacity for heightened awareness and the ability to guide souls back, it requires fortitude, balance, and, above all, a commitment to caring for the vessel and the spirit equally. If you feel called to such ceremonies, rituals, and retreats, I encourage you to do so with a Native Elder. One who has spent a lifetime communing and honoring the way of their peoples.

Sound Matters

Prior to 1970, 432 Hz was the standard tuning for recording and distribution for music and broadcasting. In the push for synthesization, the standard as changed to 440 Hz. Music went through a major shift from harmonics and melodic to heavily distorted.

432 Hz resonates with the rhythm of your heart and the natural frequencies of the Earth, aligning with the Schumann Resonance. It promotes relaxation and balance by harmonizing with the water in our bodies and the vibration of our cells. It reflects the mathematical structure of nature. Unlike 432 HZ, 440 Hz creates dissonance and tension, contributing to feelings of anxiety or agitation.

You are made of Light and Matter and your voice carries your breath– your Spirit. Therefore, Your Voice Matters! Your vessel is more than a singular unit. Every part right down to the cells and atoms is fully alive. Anything and everything can and will experience energy exchange. Being that we are roughly 70% water, and water holds memory and consciousness; we have the ability to communicate directly with our bodies.

High pitch, loud tones, rapid, and or aggressive speech will always put another on alert, *hue-man,* or *non-hue-man be-ings* alike. While soft, low tones, slower sounds are more likely to soothe and call forth other *be-ings.* Your voice has the ability to calm any situation or the extreme opposite. How you mind and project your voice carries significant weight. Mind your thoughts. Mind your energy. Mind your voice. Mind your actions.

Apply fasting to the sounds you take in, such as abrasive electrical, synthetic, and the media you listen to. There is a plethora of sound therapy you can include in your daily life such as sound bathing, daily mantras, high vibrational music, etc. Add a heaping dose of nature and being close to the water will always be the most potent.

Spell Work

When you write words out, you are "spelling" as you go. The ancients understood this. Words hold and call forth emotions and energies. We are the only animals that have the ability to create to such magnitude, and we are the only ones that create and maintain stories. It is how we communicate and manifest. Words are very potent. Spell work is the intentional practice of channeling energy and focused will to manifest desired outcomes or align with higher forces. Rooted in ancient traditions, it combines clear intent, symbolic tools like candles and herbs, and ritual actions to bridge the physical and mystical realms. Guided by the principle that energy follows thought, spell work emphasizes alignment with natural laws, ethical responsibility, and the interconnectedness of all things. At its heart, it is a sacred act of co-creation, blending thought, emotion, and ritual to transform reality and awaken potential.

Take time to journal. Write out not just your sorrows, but also your affirmations, all your dreams, aspirations and what you wish to manifest. Doing this will add to you reprogramming your realities and promoting a healthier outlook.

Spiritual Cleansings – Limpias

There are a variety of ways to clean the aura. Ritualistic bathing, cord cuttings, fire, water, and Limpias con Huevo aka egg cleanse, and smudging are my preferred methods. These methods have answered many of my prayers, assisted in the healing of others, and healed me from my own personal battles.

Maintaining your spiritual hygiene is just as vital as maintaining any other part of your vessel. There are a variety of methods to conduct a Limpia, much like molé, each healer has their own method.

Limpias are used to cleanse and purify negative energies, impurities, or spiritual disturbances. Limpias are, "curanderismo cleansing rites that can clear, heal, and revitalize the mind, body, spirit, spaces, and situations, as well as facilitate soul retrieval–recovering sacred essence energy that has left the body as a result of trauma. Limpa can also cleanse on the levels of different but interconnected dimensions, realities, and spaces." *(Buenaflor, Erika. Cleansing Rites of Curanderismo: Limpias Espirituales of Ancient Mesoamerican Shamans pg.2)*

Spiritual Herbs, Crystals, & Tools

While crystals are incredible at what they do. I want you to consider the energy and the ramifications of mining. The more you have doesn't necessarily equate to the more powerful or more protected you are. Spirituality is not an aesthetic. The deeper you go on your journey; you will find that spirituality will pull you closer to our Earth Mother. It will demand that you decolonize your mind. Really consider the sources.

The most powerful spiritual tools will be the ones that you find or what a child gives to you. Gifts from children are like those of the Creator –*Pure love.*

When you find something in nature, take a moment to ask if it is ok to take, what you intend to use it for, give gratitude and make a habit of making an offering in return. The second most powerful tools are the ones made with intentions; either with your bare hands from natural elements or one made from a healer.

You can buy pre-made anything, but will it be made with intentions and good medicine? Will it be blessed and prayed over while being made or will it be made with indifference and misery? If you must buy spiritual herbs or tools, consider buying from a native artist or another healer. You will put money directly in the hands of those who need it most, and it will be more potent.

Spiritual Bypassing

Spiritual bypassing occurs when you use spiritual practices and beliefs systems to avoid confronting unresolved emotional wounds, traumas, or psychological issues. Often as a refusal to acknowledge pain, anger, or discomfort, instead masking these feelings with overly positive affirmations, detachment, or an emphasis on forgiveness. While spirituality can be a profound tool for healing and growth, bypassing undermines its potential by suppressing authentic emotions rather than addressing the root causes. The avoidance can lead to stagnation in personal development and a lack of empathy for oneself and others. Spiritual growth requires the courage to embrace both light and shadow, masculine and feminine, integrating all aspects of the self with honesty and compassion. You must learn to be friend and quiet the monkey mind.

There is a wide variety of outstanding spiritual practices. However, you also must sit with your shadows and the shadow of the mundane world. This is why grounding, spiritual hygiene, purging and transmuting are so utterly essential. Our vessels are still of this world. You must also be aware of the horrors so that you may be able to create solutions to reduce the burning for yourself and those around you.

The only way through a storm is to head it face on. Running away will make for many repeated lessons. Confronting apathy and colonization spirits are quite challenging, as they are entangled with what we've been taught for thousands of years. You must recognize that many spiritual practices have indigenous roots. Respect is bare minimum.

Make sure you are working through your deconstruction, decolonizing your mind; and taking time to learn about their cultures and the plights of the people whom you owe your spiritual practices to. You will find that most native people need to be uplifted in some form or fashion. While you may not be able to uplift everyone, you can listen to them, learn from them, honor, and respect them and assist where you can when asked. This will ripple out like a butterfly effect. Riding oneself of apathy and indifference is quite difficult. Regardless of how difficult, stick to it. This is why you are here.

Transmute

The skill of transmuting allows you to move emotional energy through your body. Just like grass, allowing your energy body to act like a straw, you pull in energies from around you and express them outwardly. Transmuting is a skill that must be acquired and practiced often, as it will prevent the pain from making a home for long periods within your vessel. Keeping the vessel clear allows for Grace to flow through you and to all with whom your world dances with. Usually, a calm presence is all that is needed in a room for others to see more clearly. Keeping an open heart allows for creation, joy and laughter.

Do not take yourself and others too seriously. Even the Creator has a sense of humor, "Devine Comedy." Laughter allows even the densest of energies to burst through and free themselves. Relieving one's body of tension. Laughter and humor are good medicine after all. *–Laugh freely and laugh often.*

Triggers

Triggers can come in countless forms: food allergies, background noise, traumatic events, medications, specific people, or places, etc. Trauma can be direct or in-direct. Witnessing a traumatic event can be as traumatic. For example, witnessing the abuse of another and being unable to prevent it. The body does not know the difference. While identifying and addressing the multitude of triggers is tedious; the work is powerful. Shadow work aids in identifying your triggers. Your vessels contain more than just one state of *be-ing.*

Once you begin to identify, you can aid in healing those trigger wounds. You start to take your power back. Like any muscle, taking your power back takes a great deal of exercise. Avoid what sickens you at all costs, and when you cannot, prepare for inflammation. It makes the storms easier and less harsh when you are well prepared.

Avoiding triggers when possible is like having anaphylaxis. You may not always be able to prevent it, but you can keep your vessels as healthy as possible, so that when the time occurs, you are able to do so with minimal effort.

Water. Water. Water

There are a multitude of reasons why water is worshiped throughout the ages. Water is the uniting force within us all, as we are roughly made up of 75% water. From the time of conception until our birth, our infancy is surrounded by water. And when we come into *be-ing,* we are born in this world of ours, which like our body, is mostly made up of water. Just like the air that we breathe, we cannot sustain life without it. Water holds energy, emotions and memories, therefore consciousness. – *Water is Life.*

When you share with the Water like the Elder that she is, you find, like any grandmother, she transmutes the pain and gives many insights. This is what nature does so freely for all of us. Make sure you are showing her gratitude. Speak to the water lovingly, and you will find that intentional actions have the highest potential to aid and up lift.

Water gives and heals us so freely. Water cleanses and nourishes all four bodies. Water helps us to purge and transmute. Drink water as much as possible. Water naturally flushes out negative energies, lactic acid, sugars, or other toxins gently through your system.

Western Medicine & Therapy

While I do believe in the ability to heal yourself, I also recognize that modern medicine is quite a useful tool. Traditional trauma therapy is always a place to seek extra support, and the benefits should not be discounted. Frequently, they are needed to define the problem so you may seek the solutions best suited for your personal needs. Spiritual Healing and Western Medicine can be used simultaneously, and one should be mindful of negating medical research and its advances.

Chapter 13: How to Preform Ceremonies

Ceremonies can be quite formal and long winded at times. Personal Ceremonies however are specific to your life and needs. They can be altered in any way that fits your spirit and vessel. Here are a few of my ceremonies that can help you cleanse, purge, transmute, call in, and maintain. Spiritual hygiene is vital to ward off dense energies and parasites that may attach.

Colors Associated with Auras & Chakras

Take time to learn about the Chakras as it will help guide you to understand your internal energies.

- **Red:** Root Chakra: associated with passion, strength, creation, sexual energy, and protection.
- **Orange:** Sacral Chakra: Represents creativity, enthusiasm, and a positive outlook.
- **Yellow:** Solar Plexus Chakra: Signifies intellectualism, optimism, and joy.
- **Green:** Heart Chakra: Linked to balance, growth, and harmony.
- **Blue:** Throat Chakra: Suggests calmness, communication, and inner peace.
- **Indigo:** Third Eye Chakra: Associated with intuition, spirituality, and a deep inner knowing.
- **Violet:** Crown Chakra: Indicates a strong spiritual connection and sensitivity

Elements

All the elements have the ability to guide, cleanse, transmute and protect. They are our elders, and they all have a unique spirit. Treating them with reverence will strength your bound and they will come to know you in a more connected way. Speak your name to them and speak their name as well.

- **Earth:** Embodies the qualities of the Mother, stability, strength, and endurance. She aids in your ability to ground.
- **Water:** Embodies the qualities the Grand Mother, fluidity, emotions, truths and intuition. Water is by which the consciousness flows and holds memories. She aids in in nourishment and washing away *dis-eases*.
- **Air:** Embodies the qualities of the Father, communication, thought, and freedom, connected to the skies and the winds. He aids the breath that carries the essence of you.
- **Fire:** Embodies the qualities of the Grand Father, hunger for more and heart. He fuels your passion and aids in purification.
- **Lightning:** Embodies the divine spark and duality. Lightning is the same ingenious spark that makes your heart pulse and brain flood with inspiration and potential. They aid in your inspiration and action.

Left and Right Sides

Include intentional movement with your ceremonies, even if it is making a cup of coffee.

- **Left Side** is the divine feminine energy: portal for creation, empathy, intuition and healing and rooted in the ethereal world.
- **Right Side** is divine masculine energy: focus, logical, power, and forward movement, and rooted in the physical world.

How to Begin Your Ceremonies

- With any ceremony, you start with a clear and intentional mind.
- Offer Incense, Smoke or Smudge
- Humbly introduce yourself and give gratitude, intent, and prayer.
- Call in all 4 Directions(East, South, West, North), the Elements, all your Ancestors, Angels, Creator, Celestial bodies, Spirit Guides, unseen and seen forces and any other spirit you wish to honor.
- Start with Source above, to your higher self and down the ladder, through the body stopping at each chakra and energies associated, all the way down to your root, and below. Feel the energies move past your feet and deep into the ground.

How to Bathe with Ceremony

- Offer smudge or incense. Light candles for yourself and the water.
- Introduce yourself to the Water Spirit.
- Make your intentions very clear, ask the Water Spirit to assist in cleansing your energy, transmuting the density of energies that are weighing you down, and to purge them for you.
- Adding herbs, Epsom salts, or essential oils will aid in the detoxification of your muscles and ease the mind. (When using essential oils, make sure you are reading the labels. Some are for external uses; others are for ingesting. Pay attention to the suspended oil as well.)
- Choosing oils that aid in your breathing, muscles, and mind will have an increased potency. I prefer to use frankincense, myrrh, lemongrass, lavender and rose oils.
- *Emotions are Energy in motion.* Let those feelings and thoughts come in, and let the tears flow; eventually, the floodgates will burst, and they will burst forth with a deeper understanding of

your internal universe and that outside of you. The epiphanies in these moments will be the keys that set you free. In doing so, you release all that was— making the lessons and remembrance less harsh if faced again.

- As the water drains, finish your ceremony with loving thoughts towards the water. Thank her and all whom she feeds and nourishes.

How to Build an Altar

- Altars are beautiful sacred spaces, honoring ancestors, elements or deities and anything in between. It brings the act of worship into your home and into your daily life.
- By creating an altar, you are creating a ceremony. Every action that is filled with heart, intention, need, and want.
- You can use anything that makes your heart sing. Pictures, food, scarves, natural items like rocks, shells, branches, seeds, etc.

How to Collect Gifts from Mother Nature

- When finding something in nature, pause before you pick up something. Thank the Creator for showing you what you need, treating everything like it is a grandparent, a sacred child and a conscious *be-ing*.
- Tell the Creator and the object your intentions, ask if you can take it, and make an offering. Tobacco is widely used on Turtle Island, but any natural biodegradable gift will do, such as a flower or a lock of hair.
- You are offering to the Creator and Earth Mother alike. Just as you would visit someone's else home; you do not come empty handed or with ill intent, you should not take what is not yours, and you should always ask before you do so.

- Items gifted to you by the Creator and children call in remembrance as they are the most innocent and pure of heart. These will always be more potent than anything bought.

How to Control Your Dreams

- Start by having a good bedtime routine and creating ceremony for your scared space before you enter Dream World.
- Avoid snacking before bed, especially with any acidity, dense, fatty, or loaded with sugar. Include stretching or yoga before going to bed.
- Light an incense or offer smoke. Give gratitude to all 4 directions, your ancestors and helper spirits. Invite them to aid in your journey to a dream world. Ask them to guide and protect you on your path.
- Listen to high vibrational music, mantras, affirmations, low tones, or rain sound. Anything that brings your mind to peace and aids in your ability to fall asleep without too many distractions.
- Lay down and begin to meditate. Let all the stress of the day clear your mind. Ground into your body and imagine surrounding your vessel in your divine light and allow yourself to fully relax.
- As you fall asleep, start planning what you'd like to dream about, where you'd like to go, and where your spirit finds safety. This will be your anchor point. Start imagining it to the fullest detail. As you slip into the dream world, you will find that you can control your dreams.
- When you find that you are not liking what you are experiencing, you practice shifting focus. In time, you will learn to control your dreams with great ease. When you do experience a nightmare, you can simply tell your spirit to take you back to

your anchor point. This is how you traverse, dreams within dreams, within dreams.

- When you wake up. Fully stretch into your body, with the intention of calling your soul back. Give yourself a moment for your spirit and vessel to be acquainted again. Review your dreams. They will share insight, what is to come, or what you need to do for the day.

How to Cord Cut

- You will need 2 candles, 2 candle holders & 6 to 8 inches white string, salt, matches or a lighter, and an implement to carve with.
- Give gratitude to the Creator, the Fire Spirit, and set clear intentions in your mind's eye.
- Etch your name on one candle and the opposing force on the other.
- Pour salt around in your fire safe dish, in a counterclockwise motion, moving in the direction of healing.
- Place candles in the candle holder and place them in the salt. Tie the string to both candles.
- Give them about 2 inches of separation. Light your candles.
- While the candles burn, hold your intention in your mind's eye and do not let go until the candles and string are melted away. Carrying with it, the energies that bind.
- Thank the Fire spirit for assisting you in such a way. Allow each deep breath in to replenish your vessel.
- Hold your intentions for 3 to 4 days or until the energy releases.
- In this time of release, eat clean, drink plenty of water, take ceremonial baths, spend time in nature, create and do not forget to dance and play.
- When you perform cord cutting, those who you are cutting cords from tend to reach out. They sense it. Sometimes it is

through direct communication or through monitoring spirits. Do not engage. Cord cutting is absolute. If you return to speaking to those you cut cords with, it will drain you and you will have to repeat.

How to Feast the Spirits

- Like any Elder you spend time with, you listen and appreciate their wisdom.
- This is not a time to ask from the Spirits. These small moments are meant to honor them. By honoring them, you honor yourself and all of life.
- On a dish, rock, or piece of wood, give a pinch of your food and serve them first. We always feed the elders and children first.
- Share with them your love and gratitude and all the joyful moments in your life, just as you would a grandparent.
- When you're done with your meal; See them off with humility and respect.
- Give thanks to the *be-ings* for sharing a meal and time together.

How to Ground

- Hold grounding in your focus and ask for assistants from the Earth Mother and Creator to ground and transmute the energies in and around you.
- Close your eyes and take a deep breath in and slowly release. Scanning all four bodies and your environment.
- Imagine you have energy cords flowing from your hands, feet, and crown.
- Allow your energy cords to flow all the way from your feet: all the way up through the crown, and through your hands.
- Call in energy from above, moving the energy downwards until you reach your feet.

- Feel the energy moving through your feet; take slow deep breaths, and you will feel your energy move between the earth and your vessel. Allowing your energy to flow freely, deep into the earth.
- In these moments, you can share your stories, needs, and wants with Mother Earth, and quite often, the relief is so great that you are without burdens and your energy is restored.

How to Protect Your Dreams

- Give your mind an hour or more without media input. What media you do consume: choose calming music, affirmations, audio books or guided meditations that promote the mind reaching a calmer state.
- Avoid abrasive or violent images and sounds before going to sleep.
- Minimize acidic foods, sugar, heavy fats, and alcohol before sleep.
- Create a bedtime routine that also includes your personal ceremonies.
- Consider a dream catcher. Dream catchers are spiritual tools made initially by the Ojibwa Tribe, a gift from Spider Woman herself, to aid the children in their journey. They offer protection of your dreams, allowing you to connect to the dream world with ease. They catch and block unwanted parasites from attaching to your dreams.
- Dream catchers made by Native persons and intent are more potent than a dream catcher made from the box store.
- When falling asleep; review your day, what you would like to achieve, and how to achieve your plans.
- Give gratitude and invite Spider Woman in and ask her to aid and protect you in your journey to the dream world.

- When you wake up in the morning, take time to stretch back into your body calling your soul back from the travels of dream world.

How to Offer Smoke (Smudge)

- You will need: a shell or fire safe dish, sacred herb, or resin.
- If you use resin like copal, you will need charcoal pads, lighter or matches, tongs and charcoal pad.
- Place it in your fire safe dish and give it a few moments for the charcoal pad to stop sparking before placing resin on top.
- If using dried herbs, place them in your shell or fire safe dish and light.
- Place your hands in the smoke and make the motion to wash them clean. Your hands have the capacity to do great harm, and they touch everything. Wash them with the intention of good acts. Use your hands to waft the smoke over your body much like washing with water.
- Pull the smoke over your head to have good thoughts, over your eyes to have good sight, over your ears to hear good words, and over your face to speak good words, and so forth.
- Spending time in prayer in each direction will aid in your understanding of your external and internal world.
- Always close your Ceremony with gratitude.

How to Scan Your Vessel

- Scanning is consciously checking in with all four of your bodies.
- Close your eyes and have a clear and focused mind.
- Starting with the head, scan for internal and external pains. spend time with body parts and function.
- Keep it simple. Is there pain or unease? No. Keep it moving. Is there pain? Yes. Lean in and use your power of observation.

Where are you feeling it? What are you feeling? What emotions are coming up? Are there memories associated? Are they yours? Why is this coming up? How can you move them out?

- Make sure all basic needs are met. Proper exercise, nutrition, rest, shelter, and water.
- Where there is pain and discomfort, that is where you will need to focus your attention. The emotional and mental pains associated with trauma will be stored in your body as memory, and your body will not know the difference, other than to send out an alarm.
- Keep track of your triggers, as they will tell you what and where you need to focus your healing.

How to Shield- The Zipper

- Imagine your energy field is like your own personal bubble.
- Standing firm and well-grounded, take in a deep breath; bend down, holding an imagined zipper in your in the right hand,
- Make the motion of zipping your Energy up from your feet and past the top of your crown as far as possible.
- Exhaling and releasing any energies you may be noticing.

How to Perform a Limpia or Egg Cleanse

- You will need: 1 room temperature egg, two glasses, room temperature water, salt, smudge, red yarn, scissors.
- The glasses are not to be used for any other purposes, and you should not drink from them afterwards.
- Hold clear intentions
- Fill your glasses with water and a pinch of salt to one. Spend a few moments honoring the water, salt, and clear intentions.
- Speak your name to the Water and ask for its assistance to cleanse. This will be the glass you crack your egg into.

- Another glass of water will be the egg. Place it in the water for 5mins and allow it to be cleansed before using it.
- Wrap red yarn around your palm of your hand and between your thumb, so not to reabsorb any potential negative energy. Make 3 to 7 passes, cut the yarn and tuck the loose end under the rest. Avoid wrapping too tight.
- Hold the egg in your hands and thank the egg for allowing you to use its vessel and life force. Ask it to assist you in pulling all the unwanted energies out of your vessel.
- Start at the top of your crown and your third eye. Move in a counterclockwise direction all over your body, placing emphasis on all 7 Chakras, the place of discomfort, as well as the bottom of your hands and feet.
- Make sure you move from top to bottom, not up and down. You want to move the energy out. For instances you start on your shoulder, you will want to move it all the way to the tips of your fingers, not shoulder to elbow, to hand to shoulder.
- Crack the egg into the glass of water with salt and let it set for 30 minutes. You will find the more density you pull out, the more agitation in the egg white.
- Before you flush the egg down the toilet or bury it outside, ask the elements to help you transmute the dense energies and thank them for assisting you.
- The eggshell should be buried, burnt or thrown away immediately and take the trash out. Again, thank the elements and the egg for their aid.
- Immediately take a spiritual bath and again spend time with the water, allowing yourself to purge with grace.
- Keep your diet clean, laying off anything that will cause you to have an inflammatory response and drink lots of water for 72 hours.

- For more in-depth understanding, *(Buenaflor, Erika. Cleansing Rites of Curanderismo: Limpias Espirituales of Ancient Mesoamerican Shamans, pg.147)*

How to Purge with Fire

- You will need: a fire safe dish, charcoal pad & tongs, resin or sage, lighter, salt, 1x1inch paper and pencil
- Place salt in your fire safe dish.
- Hold your charcoal with your tongs, and light charcoal pad and place into your fire safe dish
- Place it in your fire safe dish and give it a few moments for the charcoal pad to stop sparking before placing resin and/or herbs on top.
- Thank the fire and ask for its assistance.
- Write down the name or parasite you wish to purge on the piece of paper, and fold in half.
- Ask the Fire spirit to burn, cut, purge, and assist in the transmutation of the energies you wish to purge
- Holding your intent in the forefront of your mind's eye, place paper on the charcoal pad.
- Follow suit with a spiritual bath. During your bath, ask your spirit guides and the water spirit to assist in transmuting all emotions that arise.
- Always thank the Spirits and the Creator when you are done.
- Ceremonies take time to integrate into spirit, mind, and body. Give yourself a lot of Grace during these moments.

Chapter 13: Closing Blessings
A Tia's Blessing

"A Tia's Blessing" - Zoila Luz Rosario Masiak 2023, was written for my children, siblings, nieces, and nephews, and for ALL I hold dear.

Remember these blessings, as our days with one another are finite and fluctuating. For we are here now and now is where we choose to be.

May you share your Light as easily as it is to drink water

— for water is Life

May the Sun always and forever shine in your favor

May you allow your Light to always shine

May you know thyself as deeply as I know myself

May you always move in the direction of the Heart

May you hold each other up

May you create Heaven on Earth and Within.

May you always support each other's desires and talents

May you seek not just the good way but a better way.

May you have more joy and bliss together, than apart.

May there always be fairness

May your voice never be silenced

May you never need to mask

May you know your truths so well that,

nobody and nothing can ever use them as a weapon against you

May you attract your soul's family with ease

May all who know you call your family with as much pride and honor as I do when I think of you

May you give birth to the creations of the Heart May abundance follow you and your beings wherever you may roam

May you never use venom with the ones you love

May you see and seek the perfection of the ALL, in each other's eyes.

–for that is where the flames of LIFE live

May you grant Grace to others with ease, and to yourself

May you lay down your armor of judgment so that

Grace may follow and flow through you with ease.

May the shadows diminish quickly within your presence, even if only when in thought

May you call your Soul back with every, "I love you."

May Apathy NOT rule your Life.

May Empathy be your strongest ally, but never Empathy without boundaries.

May you always have courage and the Willpower to move in the direction of the Heart –for willpower is the muscle of choice.

May you always choose the path of the Heart.

The Heart creates not to destroy, — nor does it belong to Self alone.

The Heart serves ALL

The Heart will always choose a better way

May hearts sing when they say your name,

–just as your name rings Harmony and Melody to your Nana,

your Mother, and I

May laughter always be your greatest attribute

Remember your sweetness

– for it is the doorway to Heaven

When it is THAT Time… Breathe in the Light calmly…slowly…with heart… With intent...

Remember these wisdoms.

Remember the joy.

Remember the bliss,

– for that is where the Heart sings the loudest

Go not in fear, but with all that you have gathered in this Lifetime.

– courage, respect, truth, honesty, humility, wisdom, and love, and above all; acceptance that you have gathered in this Lifetime.

Choose Grace

–so, you may be the embodiment of Grace Know The Now...

Every moment is Now.

The Now is where there is Life

The Now is the other doorway to bliss

For The Now, is all we ever have

All My Love,

- Zoila Luz Rosario Masiak, 2023

Resources

List A. Common Spiritual Gifts

Astral Projection: Astral Projection is where a person's spirit can leave their physical body, allowing them to explore their higher self, other dimensions, or realms. It can occur during deep relaxation, meditation, altered states of consciousness, near-death experiences (NDE), and dreaming. Ascension:

Ascension: Ascension is a personal journey of spiritual growth and evolution. It involves elevating your consciousness and awareness to higher levels of understanding, existence, and vibration. Expanded awareness, spiritual insights, and a sense of interconnectedness with all of existence and shedding your limiting beliefs. An expansion of authenticity, unconditional Love, compassion, and empathy for all living beings and promoting kindness, empathy, and a desire for liberation and the world outside of yourself.

Aura Reading: Aura Reading is the ability to perceive and interpret the energy fields or auras surrounding all living beings. This practice involves visually or sensibly detecting and understanding these energy fields' colors, patterns, and vibrations. They contain information about a person's emotional, mental, and spiritual state.

Automatic Creation: Automatic Creation is the spontaneous generation of creative works without conscious thought or deliberate intention. Allowing you to enter the flow state and connect with your higher self.

Automatic Reading: Automatic Reading is the ability to read energies without conscious thought or effort, which allows communication with the spiritual or subconscious realm.

Automatic Writing: Automatic Writing involves allowing subconscious or spiritual influences to flow through the writing. This practice entails letting words or messages flow onto paper or a computer screen without conscious thought.

Bravery: Bravery goes beyond physical courage; it pertains to inner strength and determination in times of great need. It involves the willingness to confront your limitations, doubts, and uncertainties. Bravery serves us best when you are facing great opposition.

Charisma/Charm: Charisma is the ability to attract and influence other beings naturally. The dark side of charm involves manipulation, which utilizes insincere tactics to achieve personal goals. Malevolent, energy vampires use charm to deceive and manipulate others. You must develop a keen sense of discernment so as not to fall for the tricks of those who abuse their gifts.

Channeling: Channeling is the ability to receive downloads, bringing forth knowledge into existence by transmitting messages from higher consciousness, ancestors, angels, guides, spirits, elements, nature, etc.

Clairalience: Clairalience is an ability to perceive scents or odors that are not physically present — such as smelling the scent of a loved one who has crossed over and is no longer with us in the physical world. As well as the ability to smell diseases, illness, or mal intent.

Clairaudience: Clairaudience is the ability to perceive sounds, voices, or messages not audible to the ordinary human ear. Those with a clairaudience can hear guidance from the spiritual realm, higher powers, or other sources beyond the physical world. High pitch ringing in the ears can indicate that your higher self or guides have a message for you. In the silence and when we journey within, wisdom will flood in when we choose to commune.

Claircognizance: Claircognizance or "clear knowing" involves the intuitive or instantaneous understanding of information, facts, or insights without the need for logical reasoning or external evidence. A strong gut feeling or a deep sense of knowing that doesn't come from logical reasoning or prior information.

Clairempathy: Clairempathy is a unique ability to sense the emotions of others without being told how they feel or use of apparent signs. Those with clairempathy have a heightened emotional sensitivity to others. They can notice emotional nuances, even when people are not openly expressing their feelings. While clairempathy can be a valuable gift, it can also be challenging, as it may lead to emotional overwhelm or difficulty distinguishing your emotions from those of others. Learning to set healthy emotional boundaries is vital for those with this ability.

Clairgustance: Clairgustance is the ability to receive messages, insights, or information from the spiritual or supernatural realm through the perception of taste or flavor.

Clairsentience: Clairsentience is the ability to sense energy, emotions, and information from the spiritual realm. It includes feeling subtle energies, vibrations, emotions, and spiritual entities.

Clair Observation: Clair Observation is a form of intuition that involves using all your senses to observe and interpret the world around you more clearly. Clear observation allows you to remain the observer of both your internal and external worlds. **Clairprecognition**: Clairprecognition is the ability to perceive or gain knowledge about future events before they occur. This can be through dreams, downloads, channels, meditations, or visions.

Clairproprioception: Clairproprioception is the ability to sense energy, and receive information and insights from the tactile touch, as well as the ability to pick up energy and vibration through their hair.

Clairvoyance: Clairvoyance, or "clear seeing," is the ability to perceive information, objects, events, or images beyond ordinary human senses.

Discernment: Discernment is the ability to identify, differentiate, and recognize deception or manipulation in both spiritual and physical worlds.

Divination: Divination is gaining insights or predictions through various methods like tarot card reading, astrology, palmistry, rune casting, tea leaf reading, and scrying. Involves interpreting signs, symbols, or natural phenomena to understand hidden truths or foresee outcomes. Divination practices vary from culture to culture.

Elementals: Elementals are beings or energies associated with Earth, Water, Air, Fire, and Lightning elements. These entities embody the qualities and characteristics of their corresponding elements and often play essential roles in personal ceremonies, mythologies, rituals, and personal practices.

Energy healing: Energy healing is the ability to balance and manipulate energy in the body. There is a plethora of healers who possess such qualities, and their practices are as varied as they are.

Energy reading: Energy reading is the ability to evaluate and interpret the energy field and the aura of a person, place, or object.

Exhortation: Exhortation is the gift of encouragement. Inspiring individuals to improve themselves, their communities, and society. They do so with ease, enthusiasm, urgency, and conviction, encouraging individuals to adopt beneficial attitudes and beliefs that can make a positive difference.

Grace: Grace has the power to transform our interactions with others. By embodying grace, we tap into the essence of Creation and connect with others on a deeper level. When you know grace, you come to know everyone needs grace for our peace of mind. You know it to be true that all life requires grace, as we are all children of Our Mother and Children of the Sun, both giving of themselves so effortlessly.

Healing: Healing is the ability to restore physical, emotional, mental, or spiritual well-being. Healing has just as many modalities as there are diseases. Some possess the ability to heal with their words and prayers, while others may heal with their hands.

Honesty: Honesty is the quality of being truthful and speaking with integrity. It involves being truthful, sincere, and transparent in thought, word, and action. It goes beyond simply telling the truth; it extends to being true to yourself and your spiritual journey. Honesty includes self-examination, acknowledging your flaws, and seeking to align your actions and beliefs with your core values and principles. It is knowing your authenticity, living in accordance with your true self, being genuine in your relationships with others, and having a profound connection with your higher self and the Creator and All that is.

Hospitality: Hospitality is the ability to make strangers feel welcome. It involves making others feel comfortable, valued, included, and at peace. Those with the gift of hospitality have the ability to bridge the divide between worlds.

Humility: Humility is respecting the natural world, recognizing the interconnectedness of all living beings, acknowledging the sacredness of all life forms, treating life with reverence, a willingness to learn from others, and acceptance of your imperfections. Those with such gifts understand that they are not greater or lesser than anyone else and understand the need for such balance.

Humor: Humor is a powerful gift that transmutes negative energy into positive energy by making light of a situation while still conveying truths. This tends to be the shining attribute and aspect of a Contrary Empath.

Intuition: Intuition is the ability to comprehend or perceive something without consciously reasoning or analyzing it. It is the "gut feeling" or insight into a situation, decision, or event.

Intuition is regularly disregarded as less superior than worldly knowledge; however, deeper understandings are missed when we are not connected to our inner knowledge.

Incantation: Incantation is the ability, knowledge, and practice of using words intentionally. Make no mistake, our words are indeed powerful. You can create your reality with such forces. For what our mind thinks, and our lips speak, we become.

Limpia: Limpias are used to cleanse and purify negative energies, impurities, or spiritual disturbances. Limpias are, "curanderismo cleansing rites that can clear, heal, and revitalize the mind, body, spirit, spaces, and situations, as well as facilitate soul retrieval—recovering sacred essence energy that has left the body as a result of trauma. Limpa can also cleanse on the levels of different but interconnected dimensions, realities, and spaces." *(Buenaflor, Erika. Cleansing Rites of Curanderismo: Limpias Espirituales of Ancient Mesoamerican Shamans pg.2)*

Love: Love is a gift rooted in the oneness of All that is. It is selfless and unconditional acceptance without judgment for others. It is the profound and unifying force that transcends the boundaries of the physical and spiritual worlds. A sense of interconnectedness with all living beings and the divine

Lucid Dreaming: Lucid Dreaming is a state of consciousness where you are aware that you are dreaming and can control the dreams — experiencing dreams with all the senses intact with the ability to have control of your dream state. This ability provides insights into the relationship between the conscious and subconscious mind.

Magnetism: Magnetism is the powerful ability to attract and influence others. Those who hold the power of magnetism frequently emit very bright auras, even if they themselves are unaware of their powers.

Manifesting: Manifesting is intentionally attracting or creating desired outcomes, experiences, or realities through the power of thought, belief, and intention. The ability to create your dreams through the power of attention, focus, heart, and good choices not just for yourself alone but for others.

Mediumship: Mediumship is the ability to interact with spiritual entities. Mediums communicate with the ancestors, angels, elements, guides, spirits, and other beings. They act as intermediaries between the physical and spirit worlds.

Meditation / Prayer: Meditation is a technique that involves directing the mind's focus and removing distractions to attain a state of mental clarity, relaxation, and heightened awareness.

Mercy: Mercy is a trait that defines a person with great sensitivity towards those suffering and sharing their compassion, encouragement, and providing practical help to those in need. Mercy involves being compassionate and forgiving towards people who are vulnerable, distressed, or in need. It also includes refraining from inflicting any additional harm or punishment.

Platica: Platica is a practice dating back to the Aztecs. They are heart-straightening talks that cleanse, heal, purges, renews and purifies the hearts and mind. Using the power of breath and voice with much intent. Platica for the Mexica could release wrongdoings, emotional or mental woes, and illnesses, and typically involved invoking supernatural aid. These wrongdoings, or straying from one's truth, were believed to dislocate the heart from its proper place, which could then cause disease, community disdain, or bad fortune. Straying from one's truth could encompass failing to think good thoughts, laxity in endeavors, or not being diligent in performing offerings of gratitude. Platicas could also serve as prayers or offerings to the deities and as eloquent poetic requests for absolution, purification, and aid." *(Buenaflor, Erika. Cleansing Rites of Curanderismo: Limpias Espirituales of Ancient Mesoamerican Shamans pg. 65)*

Precognition: Precognition is the ability to perceive or predict future events, experiences, or outcomes before they even occur.

Presence: the gift of presence is the ability to be fully aware, embodied, and attuned to the moment, offering healing, connection, and divine transmission through simply being. It dissolves apathy, awakens empathy, and aligns others with the truth of their own divinity.

Prophecy: Prophecy is the unmistakable ability to predict future events.

Psychics: Psychics have the ability to communicate with both seen and unseen, perceive beyond our senses, and provide guidance, insights, and predictions about the past, present, or future.

Rebirth: Rebirth is the ability to shift your consciousness so dramatically that it transforms your emotional, mental, physical, and spiritual body entirely differently from your previous self-identity. The shift is so significant even those who knew the older version no longer recognize the new version. Rebirths can occur as many times as you expand. It takes a full seven years to replace all cells in your body. The greatest shifts will be most noticeable after such time.

Remote viewing: Remote viewing is the ability to "see" distant or unseen locations, objects, or events without physically being present. It involves accessing information about a remote target through astral Projection and telepathy. It gained significant attention in the 1970s and 1980s, when the

The U.S. military, the CIA, and the Defense Intelligence Agency (DIA), explored its potential uses. Respect: Respect is the ability to honor and recognize all beings' inherent sovereignty, worth, and dignity. Having deep reverence for the sanctity of life and an understanding that we are one with all of Creation. It encompasses treating others with kindness, consideration, and fairness, regardless of differences in beliefs, backgrounds, or circumstances.

Resilience: Resilience is the ability to adapt, bounce back, and recover from adversity, challenges, or difficult situations. It involves emotional fortitude, adaptability, problem-solving skills, and a heaping scoop of humor. One of the greatest gifts bestowed to us from our ancestors is giving us the courage to keep moving forward in a time of need.

Retrocognition: Retrocognition is the ability to perceive and gain knowledge about past events without any physical connection, such as Deja Vu, historical events, past lives, or personal information.

Self-Actualization: Self-actualization is a profound process of inner awakening and self-discovery. It involves realizing and aligning with your higher self, transcending the ego and material desires, and discovering a profound sense of purpose that aligns with your spiritual path — achieving inner peace and contentment and gaining a deep understanding of the oneness of all existence. Self-actualization is a journey of inner transformation and the realization of your true nature, emotional, mental, physical, and spiritual, as we are spiritual beings having a human experience.

Shapeshifting: Shapeshifting is the ability to see through the eyes of other beings, gaining a different level of consciousness, abilities, knowledge, powers, and wisdom. Shapeshifters are known as tricksters; however, the opposite tend to be immensely powerful healers, known as the Contrary Empath.

Telepathy: Telepathy is the ability to communicate without speaking and transferring feelings, concepts, and visions from one being's mind to another without spoken words or gestures. Transmutation:

Transmutation: Transmutation refers to changing one energy into another, transforming negativity into positivity, Dark into light, and raising the vibrations of those outside of self.

Truth-Telling: Truths, or the Gift of Truth-Telling Is the ability to convey or discern spiritual truths, insights, or messages with clarity and accuracy.

Wisdom: Wisdom allows you to combine their lessons and talents and act upon their intellect and Will. It involves a deep and intuitive comprehension of spiritual and moral truths beyond mere knowledge or intelligence. Wisdom goes beyond mere intellectual knowledge and encompasses personal experiences, enlightenment and inner clarity.

Willpower: Willpower is the muscle of choice. A muscle that must be exercised and strengthened throughout your lifetime. Developing your Will requires authenticity, self-sovereignty, and a firm grasp of your undeniable personal truths.

List B. Glossary of Key Terms

This glossary serves as a comprehensive guide to the key terms and concepts essential for understanding the transformative journey described in *The Great Mass Awakening: Unraveling the Veil of Energy Vampires, Apathy, Empathy and Ascension.*

Apathy: A state of indifference or lack of emotional connection, often described as an energetic parasite that hinders spiritual growth and collective awakening. Central to the book's themes, it is identified as one of humanity's greatest adversaries.

Ascension: A multi-phase spiritual evolution process where individuals elevate their consciousness, embodying higher states of awareness, empathy, and unconditional love. This journey often involves overcoming trauma and illusions.

Christ Consciousness: A heightened state of spiritual awareness and connection embodying the teachings and essence of Christ's unconditional love, empathy, and service to others. It represents unity, compassion, and divine alignment.

Clairalience: The spiritual gift of smelling scents that are not physically present, often tied to spirit communication or energetic perception.

Clairaudience: The ability to hear messages, sounds, or voices from spiritual sources or other dimensions.

Claircognizance: The intuitive knowing of truths without prior information or evidence, often referred to as a "gut feeling" or divine download.

Clairempathy: A heightened form of empathy that allows one to feel and understand the emotional or energetic states of others on a deep, intuitive level.

Clairgustance: The ability to taste substances without physical contact, often tied to spiritual insights or communication.

Clairsentience: The gift of sensing or feeling the energy, emotions, or presence of spirits or other entities.

Clairproprioception: The ability to sense one's own or others' spatial position and movement through extrasensory means, often linked to energetic or spiritual perception.

Clairprecognition: The ability to perceive or predict events before they occur through spiritual or energetic awareness.

Clairvoyance: The spiritual gift of seeing beyond the physical realm, including visions of past, present, or future events.

Consciousness: The state of being aware and intentional with thoughts, words, and actions. Distinguished in the text from self-awareness, which pertains to understanding one's physical and mental state.

Empathy: A core concept in the book, defined as the ability to deeply understand, share, and respond to the emotions and experiences of others. Empathy is framed as a crucial skill for spiritual evolution and connection.

Energy Vampire: Individuals or entities that drain energy from others, either intentionally or unintentionally. The book categorizes various types of energy vampires and explores ways to protect against them.

Epigenetics: The study of changes in gene expression caused by external or environmental factors, rather than alterations to the genetic code itself and often linked to trauma, healing, and intergenerational patterns.

Eugenics: A pseudoscientific practice and ideology aimed at improving the human population through controlled breeding, historically associated with human rights abuses and systemic discrimination.

Light Beings: Spiritual individuals who embody empathy, grace, and service to others. Often described as lighthouses for the collective during times of spiritual awakening.

Masks: The metaphorical coverings individuals adopt to hide their authentic selves. The book discusses how masking can lead to spiritual and emotional disconnect.

Mirrors: A symbolic concept representing reflections of one's inner world and experiences in others. The book explores mirrors, including fractured and masking mirrors.

Quantum Immortality: A concept derived from quantum mechanics, proposing that consciousness persists in alternate realities, potentially explaining near-death experiences or extreme synchronicities.

Quantum Jumping: A practice or phenomenon of shifting one's consciousness into a desired alternate reality through intention, visualization, and belief.

Quantum Leaping: Like quantum jumping, involving an energetic shift into a higher state of potentiality or a significantly different life path.

Remembrance: The act of reconnecting with one's true self, heritage, and purpose. A significant step in the journey of spiritual evolution and healing.

Service to Others: A spiritual principle advocating for actions that uplift and nurture others, the Earth, and life itself. Contrasted with service to self, which is rooted in individualism and self-serving motives.

Soul Loss: A condition where fragments of the soul detach due to trauma, abuse, or significant life events. The book provides guidance on identifying and recovering from soul loss.

Spiritual Awakening: A transformative process involving expanded consciousness, emotional turbulence, and spiritual insights. This journey often begins with discomfort or "catalyst events."

Spiritual Gifts: Unique abilities bestowed upon individuals, such as clairvoyance, empathy, or healing. The book categorizes and explains these gifts as tools for growth and service.

Temporal Dissonance: The perception of differing time flow or experience when transitioning between fast-paced urban settings and slower rural environments, often tied to energetic or mental states.

The Veil: A metaphor for the illusions and barriers that obscure truth and consciousness. Removing the veil is central to spiritual awakening and enlightenment.

The Great Mass Awakening: A prophesied collective shift in consciousness where humanity reconnects with empathy, nature, and spiritual truths. Highlighted as an inevitable event requiring preparation and action.

Trickster Spirits: Entities that cause confusion, misdirection, or harm during moments of vulnerability. These spirits are often encountered during soul loss or spiritual attacks.

The Mother: A reverent term for the Earth, regarded as the source of life, wisdom, and sustenance. The book emphasizes reconnecting with The Mother as essential for survival and spiritual harmony.

The Spider Woman: A symbolic figure representing healing, creation, and interconnectedness. The author shares visions and teachings associated with Spider Woman throughout the text.

Unconditional Love: A pure, selfless love that transcends judgment and expectations. Positioned as the ultimate goal and natural state of being in the ascension process.

Vestibular Sense: The sensory system that contributes to balance and spatial orientation, plays a key role in physical awareness and grounding.

Proprioception: The sense of self-movement, body position, and equilibrium. Important for physical and energetic alignment in spiritual practices.

White Fragility: A term describing the defensive reactions and discomfort experienced by some white individuals when confronted with discussions about race and systemic privilege.

White Supremacy: A concept related to systemic and individual behaviors aimed at minimizing or erasing the contributions, cultures, or voices of non-white communities.

Types of Empaths

Animal/Fauna Empath: Highly attuned to the emotions and needs of animals, often forming deep connections with them.

Claircognizant/Intuitive Empath: Combines strong intuition with the ability to feel others' emotions and energies.

Cognitive Empath: Able to understand and interpret the thoughts and perspectives of others logically and emotionally.

Collective Empath: Feels and understands the collective energy of groups, communities, or global populations.

Contrary Empath: Specializes in recognizing and addressing contradictory energies or opposing forces in others.

Cultural Empath: Deeply connects with and understands the energies, traditions, and emotions of specific cultures.

Dream Empath: Engages with and interprets the emotions and energies experienced in dreams.

Earth/Geometric Empath: Feels the energy of the Earth, including landscapes, ley lines, and natural phenomena.

Emotional Empath: Primarily experiences and absorbs the emotional states of others.

Galactic/Solar Empath: Connects with celestial bodies and energies, including stars, planets, and the cosmos.

Historical Empath: Perceives and connects with energies tied to past events or historical figures.

Intuitive Healer Empath: Combines empathy with healing abilities to address emotional and energetic imbalances.

Physical Empath: Feels and experiences the physical sensations or ailments of others in their own body.

Plant/Flora Empath: Attuned to the energy and needs of plants and the natural world.

Precognitive Empath: Able to sense future events through emotions or energetic shifts.

Psychic/Medium Empath: Connects with spirits, energies, or otherworldly entities to receive insights or messages.

Psychometric Empath: Reads and interprets the energy of objects, places, or environments.

Sexual Empath: Perceives and navigates the intimate, emotional and energetic dynamics of relationships.

Sigma Empath: Highly independent and self-aware, capable of setting strong boundaries while deeply understanding others.

Sonic Empath: Responds to and interprets energy through sound, music, or vibrations.

Telepathic Empath: Perceives the thoughts or mental energy of others, often without verbal communication.

Healing Techniques

3-6-9 Method: A manifestation and healing technique involving focused intentions and affirmations spoken 3 times in the morning, 6 times in the afternoon, and 9 times before bed.

Affirmations: Positive statements used to foster self-empowerment, reprogram the mind, and cultivate optimism.

Ancestral Healing: The process of addressing intergenerational trauma to release burdens and honor one's lineage.

Breath Work: Controlled breathing exercises are used to regulate emotions, enhance focus, and promote energy balance.

Ceremonial Bathing: The use of ritual baths infused with intentions, herbs, or salts for cleansing and spiritual renewal.

Cord Cutting: A spiritual practice of severing unhealthy energetic attachments to people or past experiences.

Grounding: Techniques such as walking barefoot or mindfulness to anchor energy and maintain emotional stability.

Herbalism: The use of plant-based remedies for healing and balancing the physical, emotional, and spiritual bodies.

Shielding: Energy protection techniques to create a barrier against negative influences or energies.

Shadow Work: The practice of confronting and integrating unconscious aspects of the self for holistic healing.

Sobriety: Maintaining abstinence from substances to ensure clarity and energetic alignment.

Sound Therapy: Using sound, such as music, chanting, or tuning forks, to harmonize energy and promote healing.

Spiritual Cleansings (Limpias): Traditional energy-clearing rituals using tools like eggs, herbs, or smoke.

Water Healing: Engaging with water intentionally for emotional cleansing, hydration, and spiritual connection.

Works Cited

Alexander, Jean. "Changing Perspectives Now; Empathy."

2014, https://changingperspectivesnow.org/2021/03/14/empathy.Accessed 2023.

Benton-Banai, Edward. The Mishomis Book: The Voice of the Ojibway. Edited by Joe Liles, 2010 ed., University of Minnesota

Press, 1988.

Buenaflor, Erika. Cleansing Rites of Curanderismo: Limpias Espirituales of Ancient Mesoamerican Shamans. Inner

Traditions/Bear, 2018.

Degges-White, Suzanne. "Spiritual Narcissists: 12 Signs & How to Deal with One." 2023, https://www.choosingtherapy.com/spiritual-narcissists/.

Accessed 2023.

National Library of Medicine. "Vagus Nerve as Modulator of the Brain–Gut Axis in Psychiatric and Inflammatory Disorders." NCBI, 13 March 2018,

https://www.ncbi.nlm.nih.gov/pmc/articles/PMC5859128/.

Accessed 2023

Orloff, Judith. "How the Brain's Mirror Neurons Affect Empathy." Psychology Today, 28 June 2022, https://www.psychologytoday.com/us/blog/emotional- freedom/202206/how-the-brains-mirror-neurons-affect- empathy. Accessed 2023.

Psychiatric Medical Care Communications Team. "The Difference Between Empathy and Sympathy."PsychiatricMedicalCare, https://www.psychmc.com/blogs/empathy-vs-sympathy

Accessed 2023.

www.ingramcontent.com/pod-product-compliance
Lightning Source LLC
Chambersburg PA
CBHW061603120626
46550CB00004B/1604